EXPIRED MINDSETS

EXPIRED MINDSETS

RELEASING PATTERNS THAT NO LONGER SERVE YOU WELL

DR. CHARRYSE JOHNSON LCMHC NCC

NEW DEGREE PRESS

EXPIRED MINDSETS

Releasing Patterns That No Longer Serve You Well

ISBN   978-1-63676-480-1 *Paperback*
        978-1-63730-597-3 *Hardback*
        978-1-63730-383-2 *Kindle Ebook*
        978-1-63730-384-9 *Ebook*

"We may encounter many defeats, but we must not be defeated."

— MAYA ANGELOU

Contents

To My Loving Family...
Randy, Ci Ci, and RJ
You are my world and make every day worth living.
To My Mother in Heaven...
I am because you were.

Introduction

---

*"Wherever you look and see uncertainty,
look just beyond that point and open
yourself to the possibility of a shift."*

My husband Randy and I were college sweethearts. It is a miracle that we've been together for the past twenty-four years. Our first conversation was a series of me laughing and insulting his future life plans and decisively sharing what I would and wouldn't put up with in a relationship.

As we sat crouched on the apartment floor sharing our dreams for the future, I interrupted Randy and made sure he knew, "I'm only speaking to you out of courtesy. Most guys your age have no idea what they want in life, and I have no time for games." Some people might think, "Wow, she was so confident, or yikes, that was a bit much!" Perhaps, some may even believe I was a little of both...and that's all partially correct.

The semblance of confidence I had largely came from a place of defense. I was determined my life would not follow the examples of infidelity, abuse, and brokenness I witnessed as a child. If I wanted my life to be different, it meant guarding myself against falling into the same relationship patterns. I had already adopted the longstanding belief that the only person I truly needed was myself, and any man I allowed in my life would have to understand they were optional.

When I was growing up, my mom would repeatedly tell me, "I am praying for your future husband because he will have his hands full with you."

Who knew the cute college boy from New York that I gave an incredibly hard time would be up for the challenge? My best efforts to scare him away didn't work and our relationship proved to be a catalyst to my personal growth.

The intersection of our lives forced me to sit with myself and evaluate my views of strength. To embrace the present and stay open to the future, I had to sift through all of my past beliefs about men. I wasn't initially sure Randy could be trusted with my heart, but there was a comfort and ease between us that made me curious. There was also something inside that cautioned me to consider if I was standing in my own way.

We all have moments that force us to sit and reevaluate. The dynamics in our lives create an undeniable pressure that exposes the cracks in our foundation. Experiences such as uncertainty, loss, anxiety, and exhaustion erode our ability to hide. Then, without warning, this pressure can cause unresolved areas of our past to come flooding to the surface, and we decide how to respond and move forward. For some, the most challenging reality to face is that old ways of coping aren't yielding the same success; pretending to have it all together can seem like it's no longer a viable option.

When faced with disappointment and challenge, it can be easy to deny and distance ourselves from voicing the truth of our experience. We push aside unwanted thoughts and emotions, or we minimize our viewpoint, yielding instead to the opinions of the majority. We can simultaneously move through the present while hiding from our past, sometimes unconsciously walking between the continuum of defeat and toxic positivity.

I'm writing this book because I want you to know your past only holds the power you have relinquished. Our past is only meant to be a place of reference, not a place of residence. When we fully understand the importance of mindset, we can move through our struggles and operate from a place of strength.

Over the last fifteen years as a psychotherapist, educator, and consultant, I've had the privilege of helping hundreds of individuals navigate the space between struggle and strength. I've watched them step outside of their comfort zone, do the work, and experience unimaginable growth and sustainable change. It is not only a powerful process to facilitate and observe, but a philosophy I apply to my own life as well.

When I encounter individuals, who live far beneath their potential, I often find they blame their experiences instead of their effort. Some believe any sign of a challenge is a warning that failure is imminent. While others have acquired a rigid set of beliefs they carry from one season to the next believing they will replicate victory.

We operate at a level of potential that is parallel to the health of our mindset; therefore, we must embrace *the shift* within each season, choosing to face ourselves with curiosity and openness. This allows us to take an honest inventory and uncover any beliefs that are no longer in agreement with our purpose.

Through awareness, action, eviction, and alignment, the knowledge of our past can unlock our highest future potential.

Expired Mindsets will guide you through the process of

- Understanding the ROOT of your mindset and how it may be separating you from your authentic self.
- Illuminating how spoken and unspoken messages shape
  - our experiences
  - what we believe about ourselves, and
  - what we expect from others.

It can be easy to convince ourselves we've powered through our past, but in actuality, we may be carrying years of buried experiences that can keep us operating in survival mode. This state of living can then be the source of challenges such as chronic physical pain, cycles of disappointment, poor decision making, lack of confidence, and so much more.

When you reach your breaking point or decide you're ready to live differently, confronting these past points of pain will

open new pathways. You will be able to unlearn limiting patterns and create new ways to manage distress while moving toward a natural state of well-being.

As you heal:

- your individual creativity and uniqueness will have room to emerge.
- you will attract people into your life from a place of health instead of brokenness.
- you will be able to remove the barriers that prevent you from believing in your God-given power and value.
- you will learn to exercise one of the greatest powers you possess: *the ability to choose your response.*

You will love this book if you are looking for an integrative source that addresses mental health and mindset from a mind-body approach. This book is designed with you in mind, recognizing your story is unique, and the path of self-discovery is not one size fits all. It is a balanced blend of anecdotal stories, psychoeducation, and research, making it a valuable source for individuals, clinical professionals, and small group facilitators.

Traditional "self-help" books are often known for addressing a specific topic and giving you a series of steps that serve as an answer or method to solving a problem. If this is your expectation, let me invite you to push pause, but maintain hope.

When our pace moves too quickly into implementing action steps, we risk operating out of a false positive mindset. Outwardly, things appear to be better, but internally we're unable to sustain change. This makes us more susceptible to repeating emotional and interpersonal challenges we thought were resolved.

Instead of quickly giving you advice on how to feel better, I want to provide an opportunity for you to focus on the *WHAT*, the *WHY*, and the *WHERE*. To intentionally guide your awareness and insight, here are some of the tools I've included:

- Reflection questions designed for you to process **what** personal thoughts and perspectives are unfolding,
- open opportunities to use your own language to explore and reframe the mindsets highlighted,
- principles and analogies to illuminate **why** mindsets rooted in pain can block your potential for growth, and
- mindfulness activities to help you notice and track **where** your emotions show up in your body.

Turn the page and join me for a firsthand look at compelling clinical stories and relevant insight from thought leaders in the fields of mental health, mindfulness, and mind-body integration.

When you break up with the mindsets that no longer serve you well, every point of pressure can help you pivot toward your purpose. So, if you're ready to reconcile your story and embrace the shift, this book is for you.

Step from behind your shadow and honor the space you were designed to occupy!

Prologue

"Expired Mindsets: Releasing Patterns that No Longer Serve You Well"

It was the evening before my tenth birthday, and I was so excited to finally spend the day with my dad. It had been almost five years since my mom sat me on her lap and told me she and my father were getting a divorce.

Although divorce may now seem common, I grew up in a season where a divorced family was treated like a plague. Living in the South and a predominantly religious environment set the tone for judgement. Divorce was a source of shame in every part of your life, especially at school.

I would overhear teachers saying, "Please keep an eye on Charryse; her father left home and being in a dysfunctional family may begin to show up here at school."

How did my teachers even know and why was it any of their business? To add insult to injury, my peers would ask, "Did your father leave because he doesn't love you anymore?"

Early on, I didn't recognize the magnitude of those statements or even how to respond. I wasn't necessarily mad at my teachers or my friends, but I absolutely hated the way those comments made me feel. So, I tucked those feelings away.

My birthday was coming, and it would be my chance to even the score. It would be the day my father would come back into my life and prove everyone wrong. He does love me.

Keeping that thought in mind, I laid my clothes on the soft white chair in my room and hopped into bed. I slowly drifted away while imagining all the sweet things my dad would say when he saw me tomorrow.

That summer morning, I could feel the warmth of the sun shining through the window and hear the birds singing their favorite morning songs.

Even without opening my eyes or hearing the familiar whisper of my mother's

"Good morning, sweetie," I knew those sounds were my cue to wake up.

I jumped out of bed and announced, "It's July fourth and today is going to be the perfect birthday!" The outfit I chose was in my dad's favorite colors. I reached over and picked up the beautiful pale green shorts and white tank top, holding them up to my body as I ran to the mirror and smiled from ear to ear. While I began to get ready, I kept imagining all the wonderful adventures we would have today. I had no idea what my daddy had planned, but in my heart, I believed it would be special.

It wasn't long before I heard my father's brown van pull into the driveway. After spending many of my early years lying on the bed in the van, I knew that sound anywhere.

When I ran to open the door, my dad gave me the best hug ever. Oh, how I missed his hugs—I wanted time to stand still. There was something so safe and comforting about being wrapped in his arms and smelling his scent. I had almost forgotten what it was like, but in that moment, everything started off just as I imagined.

I told my mom goodbye and teased her by saying, "Don't wait up, I'm going with my daddy, and I may not ever come back." For some reason she looked concerned, but nonetheless forced a smile and told me to have a great time.

It was a beautiful day for a drive, but it didn't take long before I became bored and kept wondering how much longer it would be until the fun would begin. It felt like we made a million stops that day. Someone would walk up to the window and say, "Hey Shady Grady, what you got for me today?" Then there would be an exchange of some sort and more driving.

It took me a little maneuvering before I could figure out the exchange, and then I saw it. I knew exactly what was happening.

On the most important day in my life, my father picked me up, and we spent two-thirds of the day driving around while he carried out his drug runs. I thought to myself, "*You couldn't even make me a priority for one day.*" There were so many emotions in that moment—hurt, disappointment, anger, and sadly even a little hope.

It didn't take me long before I decided to tuck those emotions away. Refusing to give up hope, I kept telling myself at some point this part of the day will end and we will get to *me*. Yet, the more we drove, the less hope I had, and just like the sun was beginning to set, my hope was growing dim.

Finally, we stopped for food, and I wondered if this was it—the turning point. Things had to get better from here, right? I quickly get out of the car and walked toward an unfamiliar brick building with a little window and a flashing red sign that said "open."

My father reached out and opened the big, dirty green door and everyone greeted him as if he was some celebrity. A few people at a time come over and say hello, and at his prompting, wish me happy birthday. I forced a few smiles and a faint "thank you" while scanning the room to realize we're at a bar.

We sat down at the bar top, and he proceeded to yell, "Hey everyone, meet my beautiful baby girl; today is her birthday." Everyone claps and cheers, and I once again tuck away my emotions and force a smile.

My dad ordered *his usual*, then turned to me and said, "Well, no time like the present. Today I'm going to teach you how to drink so you can have your first experience with me and be safe." I stared silently in disbelief, although I had lots of ideas about how I wanted to respond. None of those ideas were nice.

I wanted to run and scream and tell off everyone in the room, but instead I remained very calm and said, "OK Dad thanks, but before we do, I just need to go to the bathroom."

What my dad didn't know is that my mom had prepared me for this moment. She instructed me to keep some "mad money" in my pocket and if at any point I get upset, call her, and she would come and get me. During my initial scan of the place, I noticed a pay phone near the bathroom.

I called my mom, told her where I was, and asked her to come as fast as possible. I told her to honk when she arrived; because as angry as I was, there was still a part of me that didn't want to hurt my dad's feelings. I hung up the phone and went and sat by my dad, pretending to have a good time.

To delay the start of drinking, I asked if I could order some fries to coat my stomach. He wasted no time getting started with his drinking, and I sat there intently listening for my mom to come to the rescue.

In what seemed like only seconds later I heard my mother honking outside. Through the smokey haze, I looked up at my dad one more time, but he was in a world of his own. I slipped down from the stool and walked out the door.

He didn't even notice I was gone, and I didn't look back.

On the way home my mind raced. I was trying to figure out how to make sense of what happened. Every emotion I tucked away was fighting to come to the surface, but I was not ready to let that happen. Somehow, my mom seemed to know just what I needed, and we drove home in complete silence. As I replayed the day in my mind, it was like seeing a puzzle with various pieces and deciding if I wanted to put them together.

By the time we arrived home, I made a clear determination. If I wanted to make it through life in a productive way, I would have to release any part of my mind that believed my father had the capacity to give me the love I desired and deserved. It was like an eternal tug of war. Up until this moment, imagining my father in my life was a means of survival. It helped me maintain a small ounce of childhood fantasy and created a forcefield around me, when people assumed I would be a failure without a father.

In that moment I knew, the very mindset that helped me would hurt me if I didn't shift perspective. Slowly but surely my mind began to slow down. The sun had been replaced by the moon and dark skies without a star in sight. I lay my head on my pillow and took a few deep breaths before the dam began to break. Finally allowing an avalanche of silent tears to stream down my cheeks, one final word came to mind.

EXPIRED.

Our Hidden Stories

_____

*The Mindset: Hiding my emotional
pain is what helps me stay strong.*

There are many different reasons we may choose to hide, dis-guise, or distance ourselves from emotional pain. Showing our emotions can feel uncomfortable and unacceptable, like a window exposing our weakness. We may be surrounded by people who exploit our vulnerability, break our trust, or even misread the symptoms of our pain.

Sometimes the responsibilities of life refuse to back down, and we aren't afforded the privilege of making our needs a priority. It can feel like the world is on our shoulders, and everywhere we turn, someone depends on us to make things happen. Seemingly small tasks can feel monumental, and we begin to think, *this may be more than I can take.*

Before long, the distance between the demands of life and the emotional cost can become so automatic we don't know how to begin the repair. The mind can move into self-preservation mode and any emotion can be a potential threat.

In these instances, our survival tactics come front and center, and we get a closer look at what we believe about strength. Sometimes, we perfect the art of making our smiles shine bright, but a deeper look into our eyes would reveal a different truth.

When I was given my mother's journals, this sentiment became even more apparent. It was like gaining the missing pieces to a puzzle I didn't know existed. My mother's choices in life took on new meaning, and I soon realized that cancer wasn't her biggest battle. Her writing revealed a lifetime of smiles, meticulously hiding parts of pain.

Journey with me through the story of her last few days because to understand her in death, you must see a glimpse of her life.

* * * *

On September 11, I was nine months pregnant, working as a fourth grade teacher and living in Frederick, Maryland, about forty-five minutes from DC. The city has long served as a major crossroads, making it a popular area for DC and Baltimore commuters.

I had just finished an extremely long day filled with anxious and tearful children who were terrified their parents would not make it home from work at the Pentagon.

As teachers, we copiously planned and rehearsed the school's emergency routines, but nothing compares to the moment it happens. That Friday, the principal came on the intercom and gave an announcement that signaled us into action. To the students, the announcement seemed standard, but as adults we knew differently.

According to protocol, the first step was to lock the classroom door. My keys were already on the beaded lanyard hanging around my neck. I casually walked toward the door and simultaneously went numb, losing my sense of feeling and resisting any temptation to think about what was happening.

My focus needed to be on protecting my students and giving them any semblance of comfort possible. This was not a drill. Mentally drifting into concerns about my family and friends was a risk I couldn't take. Survival mode was loading and everything else would have to wait.

The students read around the room, some sitting in bean bags and others stretched out comfortably on the carpet. Before I interrupted their innocence and brought them to attention, I mumbled just under my breath,

"Standards high"
"Focus sharp"
"Confidence on"
"Self-doubt off"

Telling the children about the attack on the Pentagon was one of the of the toughest things I've ever had to communicate.

I could see their quiet tears and feel the uncertainty of every child in the room. The students were eerily compliant, and worry blanketed the room like a thick morning fog.

There was a deep ache in my heart when one of my sweet students asked, "Will my parents be okay? What happens if they can't come get me?"

I desperately wanted to take that student in my arms and tell them everything would be fine, but I also knew I couldn't make that promise. Instead, my response was, "I'm sure that your parents are happy that you are safe and away from all the chaos. They are thinking about you and working to get here as soon as they can."

* * * *

Later that evening I came home to my beautiful baby girl, Cierra. She was a twenty-month-old ray of sunshine, and I couldn't wait to get one of her special hugs.

There's something about hugging your babies that makes the stress of the day melt away. I dropped my bags at the door and lowered toward the ground to make room for her embrace. As she climbed into my arms, she folded her little hands around my neck and nuzzled her head just under my chin.

After resting there for a few moments, she leaned her head back, placed her hands on my cheeks, and sweetly said, "I love you Mommy." Her words were like a key that unlocked my restraint and reminded me it was okay to breathe. I could feel my shoulders loosen and my heart begin to settle. I was coming out of survival mode, even if only for a moment.

Just in the other room, my mother, Dottie, lay on the bed battling treatment fatigue and the side effects from chemotherapy.

Over the past eight years she had multiple surgeries and several rounds of intense cancer treatment. The latest protocol had turned her tongue black and completely removed her sense of taste. She was so frail that even the smallest daily tasks, such as taking a shower, would drain her energy for hours.

Despite this reality, through all the years of battle her smile never seemed to dim.

I headed up the steps and joined my mother in watching the latest news coverage.

We lay on the bed with Cierra nestled in between our love, stretching out her little body so she could touch both of us at the same time. Our eyes were glued to the sounds and images that painfully recounted the tragedies of the day. It was sobering to think of those who had only minutes to respond, if they had any warning at all. Several of my closest friends and loved ones worked around the attacks. Thankfully, they all made it home.

Somewhere in the middle of conversation about the news, my mother's voice became weak. Speaking just above a whisper she made one final point saying, "You know honey, today people lost their lives, and they had no idea it was going to be their last, but I'm thankful that even though I don't know the time or the hour, my time on earth is coming to an end, and I am not afraid. I've done the best I can with the time I've been given."

This was a rare moment when I felt somewhat speechless. What exactly do you say when your mother is dying?

I briefly responded, "I can't imagine what they felt, and yes, you've truly made the best of every moment. I'm glad you're not afraid."

Little did I know several days later my mother would enter the hospital and she would never leave.

First diagnosed at age forty-five with stage four colon cancer, she ultimately died of metastatic lung cancer, shortly after the birth of my son.

* * * *

The day she went into the hospital began as a normal day. By mid-morning, my mother complained of some pain, which was common in this stage, but I could tell this was different. Unlike some, she didn't want to be isolated in her pain, so I immediately helped her move downstairs to lie on the couch.

Shortly thereafter, I heard my sweet baby girl through the baby monitor as she woke up from her nap.

Cierra, who was normally the life of the party, was unusually quiet that afternoon. The sound of her movement coming through the baby monitor was the only indicator she was awake from her nap.

When I reached into her crib and picked her up, she still didn't utter a word—and she was quite the talker. I carried her downstairs and headed back to the living room where my mother lay on the couch. Cierra climbed out of my arms and nestled herself right in front of my mom. You could hear a pin drop as she slowly placed the palm of her hand on my mother's cheek.

Feeling the touch of Cierra's hand, my mother opened her eyes and smiled.

She began telling me how important it would be to protect Cierra's spirit—that she was a special little girl with a big purpose to fulfill in life. In my heart, I knew my mom was beginning to say goodbye. My stomach immediately began to ache, and my heart was beating out of my chest, but outwardly I smiled and nodded in agreement.

It wasn't long before my stepfather, Lovell, was getting my mother ready to go to the hospital. Her pain had become unbearable, and it was difficult to see her suffer.

Part of me thought life was cruel. My mother had finally found love, and Lovell was her soft place to land. He was the most caring man I had ever met, and the only true presence of a father I had ever known. My mother's quality of life while battling cancer was largely due to his compassionate care.

She was admitted to the hospital that evening.

* * * *

Three days later, I finished up my school day and had a scheduled prenatal appointment. My little man was hanging tight. At almost five days overdue, we decided it was time to be induced. My bag was packed and all I needed was to choose and enjoy my last meal, then head to the hospital. I chose BBQ, and for the record, don't EVER eat this before labor!

The way the hospital was set up, I was in room 414, and farther down the hall my mother was in room 441. Checking in was smooth, and I was quickly settled in and ready to go.

The anticipation of my son's birth temporarily overshadowed my fears about my mother. Nothing was more important than having a safe delivery, so every fiber of my being yielded to that focus.

Delivery was like an episode of *The Fast and the Furious*! My body progressed so quickly that an epidural wasn't an option. Around 9:00 p.m. that mid-September evening, my sweet boy, we now call RJ, was here and healthy.

He was an angel, the perfect addition to our family, and my mother's final wish was granted. She had prayed and asked God to grant her two requests: to keep her full head of hair and to live long enough to know my son was born safely.

Two hours after delivery, I swaddled RJ and cradled him in my arms, determined to walk down the hall and see my mother.

As soon as I stepped out of the room, the nurses recommended I wait. They lectured me about the health risks of not staying in bed and taking my newborn out of the ward.

"Mrs. Johnson, we can't allow you to leave this area and put the health of you and your child at risk. Please get back into bed and perhaps you can visit oncology once you discharge."

The look on my face must have said it all because I didn't say a word, but they quickly moved out of my way.

One of the charge nurses interjected and said, "Please sign here, stating we have communicated the risks. We will take your vitals once you get back."

Without a change in demeanor and completely unfazed by the nurses' warnings, I walked carefully down the hall feeling my anxiety rise with every step. My body throbbed with pain, and I was exhausted, but determination and love helped fuel my will.

I knew from earlier reports my mother was heavily sedated on morphine and hadn't been awake for most of the day.

The door to her room was heavy and felt like trying to move a mountain. I was able to manage and quietly walked toward her bed side to gently lay RJ by her side. On her bedside tray was her chap stick, which I grabbed and began putting on her lips. She and I had this standing joke that just because you feel bad doesn't mean you have to look bad.

Between the emotions in the room and the weakness in my body, my hands trembled as I reached for her brush. I took a few breaths and let my body try and settle. God was gracious and my mother did keep a full head of beautiful hair.

I begin to brush through the soft strands and a few minutes in, SHE WOKE UP!

I think my heart stopped for a moment because I had no idea how she battled through morphine and fought her way back to coherence. Seeing her awake, one last time, was priceless.

Of course, she woke up with a smile and said, "Hi baby." I reached down and picked up RJ, so he would be in her view, feeling his warmth on one side, holding her cold frail hand on the other.

With as much strength as I could muster, I said, "Mom, he's here. He's perfect and beautiful. I will be okay, and you can let go."

I kissed her on the forehead and a few minutes later she drifted off to sleep.

* * * *

Holding RJ as tightly to my chest as possible, I slipped quietly out of the room. My legs felt like bricks, and with each step, I could feel the pain and bleeding from delivery beginning to increase.

Even so, my physical pain didn't compare to the sorrow and anguish happening in my heart.

There are no words to explain what it's like to birth a beautiful baby boy and then hours later, have your father come in and say your mom passed away.

Nothing heals the pain of living without a mother, especially one that has always been your anchor. I was twenty-five, newly married, and had two children under two.

When I was discharged, I was wheeled out of the hospital and joined in planning the funeral of my best friend.

I remember when I was younger, I would tell my mom when she wasn't on the earth anymore, I didn't want to be there either.

Here I am, still holding closely to the memories we shared, the lessons she taught, and the moments she kept hidden in an effort to remain strong.

Her journals were one of the most cherished items I received. She religiously journaled her thoughts and her prayers in the early hours of each morning. I would never hear her voice again, but at least I could keep her thoughts close. I could read about her experiences and be reminded of how she handled adversity and relentlessly demonstrated gratitude for life.

I didn't have huge expectations toward the insight her journals would reveal. Most of my life, it was just the two of us, so I had a distinct view of who I thought she was. The more I read, the more I realized how little I truly knew.

One thing was clear. My mother spent a great deal of her life battling parts of her story behind the scenes. There were parts of her nature she struggled to accept, which sometimes created a battle between her instinct and the opinions of others.

She had a quiet desire for more in life but came against road-blocks that sometimes caused her *to fall back and conform to the needs of others over her own.* In some ways her selflessness was a part of her beauty, but it also left her holding on to pain that wasn't hers to carry.

I am definitely a strong divergence from my mother's temperament. Due to her religious upbringing, she placed great focus on the thoughts and judgments of others. On the contrary, I was born with a temperament that could care less what other people think. I've always *refused to let other people put me in their box.*

Admittedly, my strength of will was challenging for my mother's sweet and compliant nature, but I'm thankful she always gave me the space to be myself. I've often wondered what it was like for her to give me the permission she couldn't give herself—but more on that later.

Like many, to honor the expectations of others, she paid a price. Decisions were made through copious inner chatter, and she gave up on dreams others encouraged her to abandon. In the end, only my mother knows if the price was too great. Either way, her life was the foundation to some of my greatest insights around our hidden stories.

* * * *

When we don't honor the fullness of our story, it influences our direction and our experiences. More importantly, it can keep us attached to people and situations that do more harm than good. Brené Brown echoes this so well when she declares, "You either walk inside your story and own it, or you stand outside and hustle for your worthiness" (2015).

Another challenge to hiding parts of ourselves is losing sight of our identity. We become an accumulation of other people's expectations and dreams, often to wake up and realize this isn't the life we imagined. This can cause us to resent our daily existence and even fear what we would lose if we stopped playing by the rules.

In this reality, there are some important questions to ask:

- What has been the cost of leaving parts of who we are behind? Of burying them deep within and ignoring the messages they are trying to speak?

Whether we choose to listen or relentlessly work to mask them, our hidden stories are interwoven into the tapestry of our being, acting as silent yet powerful messengers.

When working with clients, I often give the analogy that walking through life fractured and distanced from ourselves is like expecting nourishment from artificial food.

We may find ourselves staring at an array of colorful and delicious looking food only to reach forward and discover it is fake. This can not only leave us starved and disappointed, but malnourished and desperate for something of substance. Despite the emptiness, we may symbolically keep showing up and dining at the table of unmet needs.

Inherently, we will always seek ways to meet our needs. So many of us spend our lives searching for the magic combination of love and achievements that will bring us the peace and contentment we desire.

We think if we find the right person to love us, then we will have permission to love ourselves. Or if we make enough money to be financially secure, then we will feel safe. Yet, we can have everything and have nothing at all, caught in a loop of repeated patterns that keep what we desire just beyond our reach.

On the other end of the spectrum, there can be deep and hidden places of sadness and self-deprecation, where you have given up trying to pretend. Your aim is to beat others to the punch by being your own worst critic. Your mind and heart are constantly consumed with comparison and feelings such as jealousy, anger, and hopelessness.

Some of us exist in the space between these extremes and have only grazed these polarities, but the struggle is still very alive and well. Life is being delicately balanced on a tightrope of existence. You may believe you've found the perfect formula to happiness, and as long as you stay in control, all is well.

As we move through the chapters ahead, some of you will begin to rethink what it means to be fully seen. My hope is for you to notice if and how you hide during discomfort, perhaps believing your safest route is to mask and protect your core nature.

Here are two possibilities to the slow and deliberate act of allowing the truth of our nature to be seen:

- the right people will be drawn to our lives
- the right people will choose to walk away

For this to occur, we must operate from a firm foundation of self-worth and instinctively recognize and honor, when our needs aren't being met.

We must embrace the relentless pursuit of learning and unlearning and acknowledge growth will require both *intention* and *personal responsibility.* Discomfort holds power beyond bringing us to our knees. It can push us to abandon our outdated ways of living life.

No one can compensate for the love we are unwilling to give ourselves. We all have hidden stories that mask both our pain and our potential.

Are you exhausted by the weight of pretending to always feel strong? Do you question your potential and fear others will begin to see you the way you see yourself?

Pause...breathe deeply and notice what thoughts are beginning to rise. Each breath is an invitation—a moment of decision. For those who need it, there is a new option on the table. Own your story and explore any patterns that maintain cycles of defeat because we repeat what we don't repair.

RESTORE:

Integrating mindfulness will allow you to notice your thoughts and emotions from a place of separation and extend acceptance toward them. Here, the focus isn't on changing or replacing your beliefs. The emphasis is on noticing your internal reactions and reconnecting with your ability to choose an adaptive or functional response that honors your values and goals.

I invite you to engage in these optional activities after reading but before you move into written or cognitive reflection. You can engage in this mindful practice as many times as needed. Be patient as you learn to listen to your body and trust you'll know when you're ready to move into reflection. There is no right or wrong to how you move through this exercise. Always feel free to adapt and modify these suggestions to match your preferences.

EQUAL BREATHING:

Find a quiet space and take a moment to connect with your breath. Begin to practice equal breathing, where you inhale for the same amount of time as you exhale. Practice this experience sitting with your feet flat on the ground or lying on your back. If you're comfortable, read through the count below and then close your eyes and be mindful of any thoughts or feelings that surface.

- Slowly count 1-2-3-4 as you inhale through your nose.

- Exhale for the same count while keeping your mouth gently closed. (Repeat)

When you're ready, slowly open your eyes and mindfully consider the questions below:

REFLECT:

Unmasking is symbolic for being able to acknowledge the parts of ourselves we cover, bury, or hide. What comes to mind when you think of any invisible masks you may wear?

How well are you able to pinpoint your concealed emotional experiences? (This exploration is intended to focus on those moments that tap into a direct place you want to avoid, not the places that easily surface.)

In as much detail as you can remember, describe the earliest recollection you have of not feeling safe to be yourself.

How do your *hidden stories* influence your view of self? of others?

RECALIBRATE:

"Reframing" is a technique designed to help you consciously shift rigid and harmful thoughts and mindsets. When we practice this skill, rigid and oppressive mindsets move toward neutrality. It can be a helpful way to turn problems or negative thoughts into opportunities for change and growth. If you're ready, use the space below to begin working on a reframe that honors what feels possible for you.

From this point forward, I will use "recalibrate" to refer to the process of reframing. I love the concept of recalibration: coming back to something and noticing if it is gradually drifting off course. Shifting your beliefs is an ongoing process and will take shape through each situation you walk through.

This section will land differently with everyone. If you don't feel ready to shift into new language around a mindset, this can be a normative part of change. The goal is to move away from the rigidity of the original mindset into a "mental shift" that is more flexible and neutral in tone. It can be difficult to adjust your thoughts, so be patient with yourself and remember to use words and language that align with the context of your life, identity, and voice.

The Mindset: Hiding my emotional pain is what helps me stay strong.

*Use the space below to develop a **mental shift** statement to help recalibrate your perspective on the mindset above:*

CH.2

Voices in the Valley

———

The Mindset: Life is often a sequence of waiting for the next bad thing to happen.

Early one summer, I was talking to a sweet young lady, Karsynn, about her recent mission trip to Johannesburg, South Africa. At the time, Karsynn was in her mid-twenties, newly married, and in an introspective season of life and self-discovery. While in South Africa, Karsynn traveled to the Kruger National Game Park Reserve where she went on a safari.

As she recalled her adventure, she reminded me of a kid waking up on Christmas filled with hope and anticipation. Her hope, and one the of top priorities on her bucket list, was to see her all-time favorite animal, a giraffe.

Along the drive, she described being in awe of the territory and allowing herself to be fully present and engaged over the three-and-a-half-hour excursion. Despite her optimism, the oppressive heat made her increasingly disappointed as she realized they were nearing the end and she still hadn't caught a glimpse of a giraffe.

Karsynn asked the tour guide why they hadn't seen any giraffes, to which he promptly replied, "Oh, they are hanging out in the valley because that's where they can find fruit."

Her heart sank. She was closer than ever to making this dream come true, but it wasn't going to happen that day. As they drove along, she imagined giraffes elongating their necks and reaching into the trees to satisfy their hunger.

Unlike the giraffe, humans love the mountaintop over the valley. Mountaintops are inspiring and easily attract awe and attention; they symbolize all that we desire and the power we feel believing we are in control. The power of making it to the top can be a seductive force luring us to ignore the risk of the climb. We are often *hesitant to change direction and relinquish what we want to find what we need.*

The mountaintop can also be analogous to the moments we consider ourselves to be on top of our game, feel strong, or feel everything is perfectly in place. Embrace and enjoy your mountaintop moments, but remember they are transient, and no one can exist at the highest point forever.

In the valley of our life experiences, we uniquely discover who we are and how we navigate through difficult moments. The valley builds strength and endurance, reminding you the efforts of your climb were not in vain.

Our minds effortlessly dwell on the moments where we stand on the mountain in comfort and ease, but we often forget to process and acknowledge the significance of what we learned along the way.

* * * *

Imagine going hiking with friends. The weather is beautiful, you have all the right gear, and you're looking forward to climbing new terrain. Each step seems familiar, yet different and unpredictable as you move along the trail.

Finally, you reach the top and find the ideal spot for the perfect picture. You become incessant and determined to capture a moment that will make others look in awe, imagining it was the perfect day. Undoubtedly, the view does not disappoint, but it is a very small facet of a much bigger picture.

Not pictured are the moments of fear when the climb became steep and the way you kept pushing when the altitude made it difficult to breathe. Forgotten are the voices of friends who encouraged you to keep going when it felt like your body was ready to stop.

On your way down, still reminiscing on the view from the top, you continue to miss what surrounds you. Leafy vegetation and foliage stands in contrast to the everyday view of the streets you drive. Streams of water run over rocks, revealing how ease and effort coexist in harmony.

Uneven surfaces and exposed roots intentionally slow your pace while melting off the sedentary state that blankets your body on most days. But your head is still in the clouds, and before you know it, you're at the base of the mountain preparing to say goodbye.

Your final thought—"I can't wait to do that again."

As individuals, we spend a significant amount of time seeking to replicate our mountaintop experiences, often ignoring the growth opportunities only found in the valley.

Many of us find our strength, our passion, and our purpose as we navigate some of our most difficult moments. However, growth through difficulty is a choice, contingent on viewing our experiences as the enemy, or a lesson.

Perspective matters.

It is one of the core ingredients to the internal dialogue we maintain. If we believe in our ability to manage distress, challenging moments become bootcamp or another opportunity to mature and develop our emotional strength. We can speak to ourselves in neutrality and confidence, while pulling from the strength of our past resilience.

When we doubt our ability to defeat distress, we are often replaying every past point of perceived failure. Challenging moments are assumed threats and our primary goal is to distance ourselves from the possibility of pain. Our inner dialogue becomes filled with statements of self-doubt and every outcome we imagine is the worst case scenario.

It's not uncommon, or inappropriate, to distance ourselves from experiences that can create emotions such as rejection, uncertainty, fear, or overwhelm. The same way our immune system defends our body from a virus, our brain can dissociate from an experience. If an event or memory is traumatic or exceeds our emotional or developmental capacity, our brain will hide it, creating what we call a repressed memory (Otegar et al. 2019).

* * * *

Our brain's primary goal is survival, and when we feel alarmed, it immediately activates. If you're standing along a busy street and a car swerves in your direction, your brain will instinctively signal your body's reflexes to move and jump out of the way.

You'll feel a surge of adrenaline shoot through your veins, your heart rate will increase, and as you return to a feeling of safety, thoughts of gratitude and calm will emerge.

Without these reactions, we would overlook harm or the ability to sense threat. So, while we often view fear as an emotional villain, it is also necessary in keeping us safe.

While I don't want to take you too deeply into the neuroscience of the brain, some basic education can be vital to understanding your thoughts, emotions, and behaviors.

Trauma scientists have discovered the brain is made up of three parts: the reptilian, sometimes called "lizard brain," the limbic brain, and the neocortex. Each of these areas of the brain play a part in our response.

The lizard brain is reliable, yet often rigid and compulsive. It involves your primitive drives related to appetite, sexuality, habits, and procedural memory and controls our "fight or flight" response. Have you ever made an impulse buy and then, moments later, you were filled with regret?

This part of our brain is highly involved in our consumer decision making, so next time you get in trouble for shopping, tell your spouse, "My lizard brain made me do it!"

Or better yet, learn to tap into your limbic brain that holds the values and judgments you make that influence your behavior.

The limbic brain holds the center of our motivation, emotions, and procedural memory. It holds the automatic routines and patterns we engage in without much thought. I hate to burst your shopping bubble, but you can use this part of your brain to delay immediate gratification and stay within budget.

Then we have the neocortex which holds a vast amount of flexibility, enables language, abstract reasoning, imagination, and our ability to develop (Barlow, Durand, and Hofmann, 2018).

This is the largest area of our brain and the seat of our consciousness. It's like an electrical grid that keeps everything in order. If it is damaged through head trauma, we would struggle to engage in actions such as writing, speaking, and interpreting social cues.

* * * *

New insights come into consciousness at any point in our lives. These moments can be the result of our intentional efforts to reconcile our past. There can also be unexpected moments when fragments of our past appear without welcome.

Let's consider the details of a pivotal moment that occurred during my late teens.

[Before you read further, please note the theme of this story involves content that may be activating to some. Pace yourself, and if at any moment you feel overwhelmed, skip down to the marked line below.]

I was a seventeen-year-old senior in high school when I began experiencing repressed memories.

It was still extremely hot in late August, so I decided to switch up my normal after-school routine of hanging out with friends and head straight home to soak up some AC. Even after years of being a latchkey child, I still had an aversion to walking into an empty house.

Don't get me wrong—I love my alone time—but sometimes it felt like countless hours until anyone came home, and I didn't always feel safe by myself.

I laughed to myself and decided to turn down the thermostat while no one was home. Someone would eventually come and turn it back up, but I would delay melting from the heat for as long as possible. No one will ever convince me that your home feeling like a sauna saves that much money.

Even though I had the house to myself, my room was my little slice of heaven. My school bag was thrown on the floor, which I sat on with my back against the headboard. As I scrolled through the television channels, I paused on an episode of the *The Oprah Winfrey Show*.

I wondered why people watch these shows. How could anything of value be learned from a talk show? The guest of the day was a psychologist talking about childhood experiences and how they can be hidden from the mind. He mentioned that these hidden experiences can show up in fragments through our dreams. This piqued my interest, so I watched for a few more minutes before drifting off to sleep.

Unaware of how much time had passed, I became startled and abruptly woke up. The house was still nice and cool, but I felt feverish and clammy.

Within what seemed like seconds, the images from my dreams had followed me into reality. My heart was beating a million miles per hour and my mind was in a tug of war between the pictures coming to the surface and the version of the truth I wanted to believe.

It was as if I was looking down and seeing a picture of my five-year-old self. It had been twelve years since leaving my childhood home, which was nestled in a friendly neighborhood that backed up to the community ball fields.

Just before I turned five, my parents were still together, and life with them and my older siblings seemed predictable and carefree. Yet, some unforeseen details became painfully clear.

The entire layout of my first childhood home, came back to my memory—the colors, the rooms, the furniture, and the hidden stories I didn't know I was carrying. Time of day was not something I could recall, but there I was, lying in a dark room, frozen still. The door opened and he walked in…

Why wasn't I moving? Why didn't I resist or even scream out? I could see the crack of the light under the door and the voices of my family as they passed through the hallway.

Years of memories of childhood sexual abuse came flooding to the surface. Once again, I found myself paralyzed, numb, and in shock. How could someone who was supposed to love and protect me hurt me? And now that I remember, what do I do with this information?

Once I recovered from the physical sensations overwhelming my body, my thoughts felt like countless stars hiding in the night sky. There I was, thrust deep into the valley, alone and reliving the details of traumatic memories experienced in childhood.

I wondered what shifted and gave my mind permission to bring that memory to life. What good would it do to remember something so awful?

Even today, these questions remain unanswered. The door was opened to that point of pain, and I was the only person who could choose the way forward.

I believe something about the timing was providential. It was like being at a fork in the road and choosing to face what had been revealed or choosing to deny it was real.

It's never easy to acknowledge sexual trauma. Actually, prior to this moment, I can count on one hand the number of people who know this story. But telling you is important. It feels right. I am placing myself in the vulnerability seat because I want you to know, as a passenger, I'm also sharing from a place of lived experience.

* * * *

Repression is an automatic process that occurs when an experience is so overwhelming, the mind subconsciously blocks the memory as a means of protection. Suppression is voluntary and involves a conscious choice to forget unwanted thoughts and experiences (Barlow, Durand, and Hofmann 2018).

Let me also add, what our mind chooses to repress is subjective. You may not have repressed experiences of this magnitude, but even "lighter" memories can have significant influence on your mindset.

Several years ago, I was working with a client, Greg, who kept recalling a summer at his grandparents' house. He could never make strong social connections with any of the kids in the neighborhood.

To some, this may not sound like a big deal, but over time, Greg realized that experience translated as rejection. It caused him to move through life feeling inferior and like he never fit in among his family or friends.

It is both our conscious and subconscious thoughts and experiences that frame our inner dialogue or our voices in the valley.

In the midst of valley experiences, our internal thoughts can be difficult to recognize. They may seem to change by the minute and at times feel like they're speaking in a foreign language. It's important to know they exist and to *learn the unique way they show up in your life.* Not your friend's life, not your partner's life, or the life of your favorite podcaster, blogger, or social media influencer.

* * * *

Throughout life, you will have multiple valley experiences, and regardless of who you are, your beliefs and your level of affluence choose to listen to them. Over the years, I've researched and explored the power of our thoughts and the way they may emerge as themes that give voice to our mindsets. While no exhaustive list will ever be created, I invite you to explore the *voices in the valley* I have identified below:

VOICE OF DOUBT

One of the most challenging aspects of our valley experiences can be questioning the validity of what we feel. As I recalled my own valley experience with sexual abuse, I questioned if it happened at all.

For months, I went back and forth and wondered if there could be another source for the feelings and images that surfaced. Was I personalizing part of a movie I watched or another story I heard? My abuser was still a constant figure in my life. They were family and I still cared for them. The voice of doubt was loud and made me question why I wasn't angry and if perhaps it was somehow my fault.

A healthy dose of self-doubt helps us recognize we are not always right, but in a chronic state, it is dangerous. When the voice of doubt is too active, it steals your confidence and challenges your intuition. It often partners with anxiety and fear, becoming a formidable foe to your overall health and well-being.

Doubt must be conquered at all costs. Your ability to trust your truth is an innate safety mechanism, but when overshadowed by doubt, it leads to endless patterns of indecision and low self-esteem. It cuts off our natural ability to validate and examine our responses with confidence and clarity.

VOICE OF SHAME

Shame can be another all too familiar voice when we recall or walk through our valley experiences. I was amazed at the level of shame that took its opportunity to speak. Logically, I knew the abuse I endured couldn't have been my fault, yet there was a resounding internal voice steeped in shame that was reinforced by my silence and secrecy.

One of my first thoughts was to keep this newfound discovery to myself. If exposed, it would destroy the dynamics of my family and in turn extend the depth of shame I felt.

Shame is draining and takes so much energy to keep hidden. It can be caused by experiences such as feeling we allowed ourselves to be manipulated, not performing up to the expectations of others, regret over past choices we've made, or even how we look.

The voice of shame can be powerful, causing us to feel defective, damaged beyond repair, and downright unworthy. It is sneaky and can hide itself through mindsets such as denial, distraction, defensiveness, and anxious avoidance. At its worst, shame drives our behaviors and leads us to believe emotional disconnection is one of the best ways to maintain our secrets.

Studies have shown the fear from shame can shut down the higher-level functions of our rational brain's cognitive processing (Michl et al. 2014). In other words, our lizard brain ignites, reasoning goes out the window, and a level of vulnerability occurs that can open the door to impulsivity, destructive behaviors, and addictions.

VOICE OF DEFEAT

Feelings of defeat can be quite subjective and often manifest through the personal recipe of our lives that are already in place. Once the fragments of my memories surfaced, the voice of defeat taunted me and brought waves of powerlessness and overwhelm. It was like a switch that someone had broken so you could never turn it off. Defeat, sometimes whispering and other times yelling, attempted to deflate my natural sense of hope and optimism. I was terrified of future intimacy and now wondered if I would be able to appropriately welcome touch.

The voice of defeat can be like a leech, attaching to your spirit like a parasite feasting on your vulnerabilities. If we don't silence defeat, it can manifest into victim mentality. We can become allies with our pain and use it to validate our unhealthy mindsets and patterns of response. For instance, we can use it to justify not trying since we unequivocally believe we will fail. Defeat can also speak from a place of deception, leading you to believe you have the right to complain. You become the victim of every circumstance.

The voice of defeat convinces you every valley ahead will be catastrophic. In my case, I could have moved toward a nature of aggression to ensure I was perceived as so tough that no one would ever dare touch me again. When the voice of defeat is primary, you resign to the belief life will always be bad. Consequently, your existence can be reduced to waiting for the next bad thing to happen.

VOICE OF SURRENDER

Surrender is often viewed as failure—a last resort that signals we should give up because we will never win. However, when the voice of surrender shifts from elimination of threat to illumination of our strength, something powerful can happen.

This voice is not a white flag telling you to give up and be taken captive. It is a soothing voice, always occurring in the present and rooted in your places of strength.

The voice of surrender encourages you to yield without fear and to look beyond what you see. It gives you the courage to decode the hidden messages masked behind the chatter. It is a chance to accept and process your painful experiences through a lens of nonjudgment.

Looking back, I can't pinpoint the exact moment I could both hear and yield to the voice of surrender. It didn't happen overnight, but slowly and surely, it came to the rescue.

When we do the work, the voice of surrender builds like a crescendo. While it may initially be inaudible, each time we face the voices in our battles, we create the space for surrender to build and take its rightful place.

Many of us walk through valley experiences and want them to end as quickly as they began. Some of our most difficult valleys are the ones we don't understand and those that equally seem to be surrounded by land mines. Our steps can be filled with fears and the slightest amount of pressure will create an explosion. But let me reinforce one final perspective:

The valley is not meant to crush you, but to teach you invaluable lessons you would not otherwise learn.

They are a purposeful time of preparation filled with critical choices that can transform your mindset and prepare you for your next mountaintop experience. So, whether you find yourself entering, walking through, or exiting a valley experience, breathe.

The valley is temporary.

RESTORE:

TRIANGLE BREATHING
For this exercise, use the pointer finger on either hand.

Start at the bottom left of the triangle. Breathe in for three counts as you trace the first side of the triangle.

Hold your breath for three counts as you trace the second side of the triangle.

Breathe out for three counts as you trace the bottom side of the triangle. You have just completed one deep breath.

[Repeat this sequence three to five times or until you begin to feel an increased sense of grounding.]

REFLECT:

Your internal dialogue is your thoughts—the part of you that comments on every aspect of your life. It gives us the ability to reason, but depending on the language we use, it can be both helpful and unhelpful.

What have you noticed about the way you speak to yourself?

Which voice in the valley is most prominent when you go through difficult times?

How have your past experiences positively or negatively influenced your internal dialogue?

What do you think your internal narrative says about the current state of your mindset?

RECALIBRATE:

The Mindset: Life is often a sequence of waiting for the next bad thing to happen.

*Use the space below to develop a **mental shift** to help re-calibrate your perspective on the mindset above:*

The Iceberg Illusion

---

*The Mindset: Burying my pain
protects those I love.*

It was mid-December, about three months after my mother passed away, and the thought of spending the first Christmas without her was brutal. For as long as I could remember Christmas was our favorite holiday.

That year, nothing felt cheery and bright and the thought of doing anything beyond breathing felt insurmountable. Whether we were in a season of plenty or a season of adversity, my mom had a way of making it special. She was the magic of the season and kept our family focused on the joy that comes through giving.

There were only two weeks until Christmas, and every day since Thanksgiving, I told myself I would pull it together and decorate the house ready for Christmas.

Instead, I would wake up, walk down the steps, and try my best to avoid looking in the living room. I couldn't bring myself to open the boxes of decor stacked in the corner. Every time I went near them, I would begin to feel jittery and teary, as if I was going to lose my breath. In my mind, opening the boxes would be like an emotional tsunami, and I wasn't confident I could survive another storm.

On the bright side, being a young mother gave me the focus I needed to keep at least one foot in the present. It forced me to stay calm enough to nurse and every few hours I knew a child needed to be fed, changed, or given some attention.

In the back of my mind, I also knew I *could* skip Christmas and my kids were small enough they wouldn't remember.

About a week before Christmas, my mother's older sister Lillie reached out by phone. My habit at that point was to immediately decline calls, but something encouraged me to answer.

I always loved the sound of her voice. It was warm and confident, and she was also one of the funniest and most spirited people I knew. True to her nature, there was a negligible amount of small talk, which I appreciated, and she moved right to the point.

"Honey, I know this is hard, but you can't give up. You have a sweet little family that needs all of you, and they will know if anything is standing in between them and your heart."

I was deciding whether to reply with honesty or pretend I was fine, when a few silent and salty tears began sliding down my cheeks.

After giving myself a few more seconds to breathe, I cleared my throat and replied, "I hear you, but is it really that big of a deal? Everything that made this season beautiful is now gone, and it will never be the same."

My heart braced for what would come next and my aunt's response pierced through to my heart: "Yes, Charryse, it won't ever be the same, but your family should never pay the price for the pain you carry. One day in the future, your children will look back and want to see pictures. Your baby will ask questions about his first Christmas. When that time comes, what do you want to say? And how will this year honor what your mother has poured into your life?"

Every ounce of me immediately decided the conversation was over: "Thanks Auntie, I will keep that in mind. I appreciate your call and I will talk to you soon."

What in the world?! Now filled with anger, I quickly hung up, and despite what I said, there was nothing about that call to appreciate. As a matter of fact, *why did I even answer the phone?* I didn't see any of that coming and the last thing I needed was more pressure.

Grief should be off limits; didn't she know that? Everyone else followed the rules: leave me alone and let me handle things my way, by burying the pain until it is no longer a threat.

My immediate reaction was to ignore my aunt's plea, but after spending most of the day replaying the conversation in my mind, the thought of not celebrating the season seemed as dishonoring my mother and over the top.

My aunt had recently lost her youngest sister and perhaps she was speaking from her own point of pain.

I was about to call a friend to cosign on my opinions, when I had an epiphany and figured out what my aunt was trying to convey.

It was not about the material aspects of the season. It was about not letting my grief take root and helping me ***understand how my short-term choices could create long-term consequences***. This can be difficult to keep in perspective, especially when our protective choices seem fairly harmless.

* * * *

Choosing not to actively engage in celebrating the season would have granted me the permission I wanted to stay as numb as possible. No one would have blamed me, and for good measure, I could have added being overwhelmed and exhausted as a new mom.

Prior to that phone call, I had already planned what I would allow people to see.

Like a mighty iceberg, the goal was to outwardly show the acceptable signs of grief that would make others comfortable and keep them from looking below the surface. Instead, I was feeling the discomfort of my aunt tipping my iceberg.

The "tip of the iceberg" often refers to a small part of something that is seen or known, in relation to a much larger problem (Merriam Webster College Dictionary 2021). In my case, the desire to isolate was only a fraction of the magnitude of my grief experience.

American writer Ernest Hemingway coined a writing technique referred to as the iceberg theory or theory of omission. This writing style focuses on showing very little context or interpretation, instead encouraging readers to engage with the story in a way that the weight and gravitas of a character is only found through looking beneath the surface (Daoshan and Shuo 2014).

This theory has been translated into the field of psychology, often applied to understanding the mind and interpersonal systems, providing a simple yet valuable analogy to demonstrate how we bury our pain (Green 2019).

Symbolically, the iceberg is

- a mutual illusion we keep with both ourselves and others.
- a surface of conscious thoughts and behaviors we *allow* to be seen.

When we look beneath our iceberg and break through the barrier of the water, it enhances our ability to see. It gives us a closer look at the experiences and beliefs that secretly influence how we approach life.

Some of us will find it easy to notice and recall our hidden stories, such as an embarrassing moment, unexpected change, or missed opportunity. There will also be moments we recognize an event, but we haven't grasped, or allowed ourselves to grasp, the way it has impacted our lives.

Experiences we acknowledge as significant life markers can also happen outside our developmental maturity. They can occur during ages when we developmentally lack the emotional tools to view a situation through a multi-perspective lens.

Let's say a child is emotionally neglected by a parent who is physically present but emotionally unavailable. The child may believe the neglect reflects their worth and proves they aren't good enough to receive love. Depending on the age, children in this scenario would struggle to consider other reasons their needs aren't being met. This becomes a threat to developing a healthy self-image and sets the stage for insecurity to develop.

Later in life, this dynamic translates into adults who may use "push through" mentality as a means of setting themselves apart and demonstrating their value. Despite what they accomplish, they may consistently struggle to be content and secure in their connections with others. They may resort to burying their pain, believing that perfection and acknowledging their hurt can't coexist.

* * * *

In my life the sudden death of my mother brought me face to face with a new revelation around the ways our lives were intricately interwoven. She was both the anchor that kept me centered and the umbrella that protected me from every storm.

Growing up without a father, she was the only piece of my life that ever meant home. When life threatened to be more than I could handle, my mother was my soft place to land.

Losing her left me unprotected, vulnerable, and uncertain I could go on without her. It shattered my world and severed the most secure attachment that had ever been present.

Let me also acknowledge, the loss and disappointment caused by a living parent can create a parallel experience. When a parent is unable or unwilling to provide the connection we need, there is a sense of emptiness and hurt that can seem impossible to resolve.

Despite the ways in which they may repeatedly fail, something about our relationship with our parents hangs on and hopes it will get better. Whether you still hang on by a thread or grieve reality, I salute your efforts. Our parents play a significant role in the formation of our iceberg, often intertwining our acceptance of them with accepting ourselves.

Symbolically, our unique paradigms form from the bottom of the iceberg and up. The base of our iceberg holds our primary core beliefs. These beliefs initiate from the moment we are born and begin the process of bonding with those who provide us care (Asamen, Ellis, and Berry 2008).

Before we acquire language, our environment dictates how we respond to distress and whether we can trust our needs to be met. Then as we mature and accumulate different experiences, our perceptions build and expand, becoming positively and/or negatively reinforced (Devine and Hughes 2019). If our early life experiences allow us to express emotion in a nonjudgmental environment, we are more likely to develop confidence and trust in our ability to move from disruption to equilibrium.

On the other hand, if early experiences occur within strict and judgmental environments, individuals are more likely to battle anxiety and fear of failure and have limited confidence in their ability to maintain emotional balance.

In my work with clients, I will often ask them about the family dynamics and situations surrounding their birth. Most are unaware and even unsure how this information can have value. If your parents or other close loved ones are willing to be open and honest, find out the details of your birth story.

Push for the full details, even the aspects your family may want to keep hidden. This is the foundation of your own iceberg and may give you new insight into how you navigate the relationship with yourself and others.

We typically ask about our birth story if and when we have children and want to know what to expect. I realized that due to my mother's battle with cancer, I never had the chance to ask about my birth.

I am still processing the magnitude of what I discovered when I reached out to my siblings. In the years leading up to my birth, my parents were not doing well. The marriage had always been strained and perhaps was growing worse.

Due to the physical abuse at the hand of my father, my mother endured four miscarriages. She had resigned to the fact another loss would be dangerous and at the recommendation of her doctor had her tubes tied.

After being told she was pregnant, I can't imagine the conflicting emotions that surged through her body. She was anticipating the grief and trauma of another loss. The doctor also cautiously reminded her of the condition of her body and that all symptoms pointed to an ectopic pregnancy.

Approaching her thirties, no one believed it was in her best interest to be pregnant or that her body was strong enough to sustain life. She could have chosen to mitigate the risk and expel the pregnancy but decided to let it all play out.

Against all odds, she carried me to term. We both survived.

By the time I was born, my three older siblings were between the ages of seven and nine years old. My sister, Andrea, then the youngest, thought she had sealed the deal on being the baby.

Surprise! I was born on July 4, the day before her birthday.

While I grew up thinking this was hilarious, my sister Andrea didn't share the same sentiment.

She spent much of my early life playfully trying to convince me I was found abandoned by a dumpster. I can see why she would be mad, but don't worry, Andrea got over it and now she loves me more than life (yes, I am totally being the bratty baby sister here).

These are the CliffsNotes to my birth story, to give an idea of the type of information you can seek out.

The origins of my story aren't picturesque, but truth always holds relevance and significance unfolds over time.

My birth didn't change the state of my parents' marriage, but the timing kept my mother going as my siblings grew older and moved out. I was a "fighter" born on Independence Day and now helping people experience emotional freedom is a primary source of fuel in my life.

Every aspect of your story has purpose, even the parts that may bring disappointment or pain.

* * * *

Pain is both relative and subjective, but something we all experience. Our individual level of tolerance and the context of our lives affects how much we can handle.

In parallel, the layers of our identity influence our beliefs toward exposing our emotional or psychological pain. Areas such as culture, gender, religious traditions, and family dynamics influence how we express and work to manage painful experiences (James and Gilliland 2017).

Growing up the unspoken message was to carry your pain from one moment to the next. Successfully moving through challenges meant you were strong enough to shoulder the increasing demands of life. My family of origin's iceberg could be summarized in two words: *Keep Pushing.*

This was often the only option because the amount of time between one trauma to the next was unpredictable. We each learned to perfect our individual version of push, and my version meant learning to internalize my emotions.

On the outside looking in this has been perceived as courage and resilience, but in truth, pushing through is rarely the best option.

The residue from unwanted encounters can manifest physically, psychologically, or emotionally, creating a sense of loss and challenging our ability to find and sustain meaning in life (Tossani 2013). We can work in connection with our body, which we will explore in later chapters, and notice when it points to unresolved areas in our lives.

Beyond the natural exhaustion of my roles as an educator, wife, and mother, I could physically sense when *pushing through* was taking a toll. My limbs became heavy, and it would feel like I was walking through water. My breathing felt shallow and labored and relief was equated with exposing the undercurrent of my emotional pain.

When *push through mentality* is the primary response, we may find ourselves:

- diminishing the magnitude of the challenges being faced,
- becoming highly critical of ourselves and our perceived inability to meet life's demands,
- with an increased need for control,
- incessantly staying prepared for the next challenge, and
- minimizing the physical and emotional signs that exist.

Pushing through is founded on the belief that life rarely allows us time to manage every obstacle that comes our way. Making decisions to survive the moment is the most viable option. Delaying decisions or allowing them to become too emotional is a threat to being prepared for the next issue life will bring. Shifting away from this mindset can be challenging but highly beneficial. This shift initiates when we place focus on where we can exercise choice and abandon wasted effort toward areas outside our control.

* * * *

The birth of my son proved to be providential and challenged my automatic habit of pushing through. Caring for my family created a daily sense of meaning, but underneath my iceberg there were conflicting mindsets at play.

I had a beautiful little girl I loved but hearing her call me Mom also felt like fuel to the fire of grief I carried. It magnified my experience of loss and equally left me with a deep sense of guilt. This was an unknown aspect of grief—the heaviness that desired to push away a small and innocent child. It was an experience only few will understand, and it had nothing to do with my love for my daughter.

As a mother, I wanted to be strong and distance my children from who I could be when overwhelmed with sadness. Yet, that seemed impossible during an age and stage of life where my children needed me for everything. Would I "push through" or initiate a level of vulnerability that would eliminate the need to maintain the illusion at home?

Children are highly sensitive beings and better attuned than we give them credit for. My beautiful Cierra, at less than two years old, could sense the waves of my emotions. When grief blanketed my personality, she would come and sit close, using some small gesture of touch to keep me present. Then almost instinctively she knew when I needed to smile and would put on a performance that to this day goes unrivaled.

My son, Randy, had a sweet and calm demeanor. Spending those days and hours holding him skin to skin was like a magic force field against despair. In a way unlike anyone else could, my children saved my life.

Under the surface of my iceberg, they gently swam according to my rhythm, never once forcing me to climb to the top and pretend I was glistening and strong.

Looking back, I now realize my aunt's phone call helped protect the undercurrent of my children's iceberg formation.

She was the life vest that helped me resist the wave of grief threatening to pull me under tow. Burying our pain is like fighting against the current and being overtaken by exhaustion before we reach dry ground. The current is best managed when we conserve our energy and do our best to stay calm.

Pushing through is overrated.

RESTORE:

THE GROUNDING CHAIR

Sit down in a comfortable chair that allows your feet to touch the ground. For those of you not gifted with height, another option is to lie on your back with your knees bent and your feet flat on the ground. The goal is to find a posture where you are comfortable and can feel the contact of a surface that supports you. If you're comfortable doing so, close your eyes or come to a soft gaze and begin to focus on your breath.

- Breathe in slowly through your nose for three counts.
- Pause briefly and hold.
- Breathe out slowly through your mouth for three counts.

Return to your normal pace of breathing and draw your attention to your body. Begin at the top of your head and imagine a light that slowly scans through each part of your frame. As this light scans your body, imagine that it melts away any heaviness you carry. If a full body focus is overwhelming, try turning your attention toward one part of your body that holds tension or discomfort and focus there.

Repeat (as desired).

REFLECT:

Think about the way your family handled difficult issues and/ or experiences when you grew up. What do you remember about these family patterns?

In what ways have you maintained these family patterns?

In what ways have you chosen to separate from these patterns?

How does the context of your life and identities influence your beliefs on addressing your emotions?

RECALIBRATE:

The Mindset: Burying my pain protects those I love.

*Use the space below to develop a **mental shift** statement that will help recalibrate your perspective:*

Tipping the Iceberg

———

The Mindset: When I don't live up to what people expect, I feel like I've failed.

I remember the day I decided to voice my thoughts and said, "Oh my word mom! Why don't you just make a sign and say come inside, stay, and take what you need. Do we have to help everyone?"

After she finished shaking her head and laughing, she replied, "Yes. To whom much is given much is required and if it's within our power to help those in need, why would we not."

For a moment, I stood there speechless. A smart comeback didn't seem appropriate.

"I think I understand. No matter how much we seem to have, there's always enough to share."

"Yes, that's the point."

Faith and spirituality were foundational aspects to my mother, Dottie's, beliefs. One of her core motivations was to show unconditional love and acceptance to everyone she met. She enjoyed meeting the tangible needs of those around her, which as a child I didn't always understand or appreciate. If we had extra space in our home, it was always open to those in need.

What always amazed me was my mother's ability to remain hopeful. Throughout her experiences of divorce, loss, rejection, and abandonment she remained softhearted and selfless. Her composure was a master class on peace, and she naturally shied away from unnecessary confrontation. She never sought the spotlight, but when she entered the room people were drawn to her countenance.

Her hair and nails were always well kept and in perfect harmony with her attire. Even when dressed to the nines, she didn't miss a moment to have fun. In one of my favorite pictures, she hangs on the monkey bars and laughs while wearing a black pencil skirt, long sleeve white blouse, and heels!

When she smiled, it filled her face, and I loved the way it made her eyes slant at the edges. It was as calm and beautiful as a morning sunrise and pierced through when seasons of life would attempt to steal her light.

* * * *

My mother's journals were inspiring and shifted my perspective on some of the core areas of her identity. Her spiritual conditioning was a double-edged sword. In adversity, her faith was a source of strength and resilience that exceeded what I knew of her basic nature, which often sought to please. An undercurrent of rigid religious expectations mixed with her empathy would sometimes hinder her willingness to acknowledge her needs. She would stay in personal and professional situations that were unhealthy, shouldering the actions of people who manipulated her kindness.

When I was in the sixth grade, my mom switched from working days to third shift. Each night she was at work by 11:00 p.m. and her shift, intended to end at 7:00 a.m., often extended until eight or nine o'clock in the morning. Working this shift increased her earning potential and allowed her to be at home with me after school.

Prior to this change, I came home to an empty house and entertained myself until around six o'clock in the evening when my mother arrived home. We would not only have much needed time together, but our financial situation would significantly improve.

Excited to no longer be in a place of constant struggle, small shopping excursions became a part of our weekend ritual. Unsure of how long these freedoms would last, I took full advantage of my newfound passion for retail therapy.

Oh, wow, reconnecting with this memory makes me laugh. I am currently a devoted member of the "Amazon Fanatics Club" and still enjoy retail therapy a little too much! But we will come back to that connection in the chapters ahead.

"Hey Mom, you okay? You look like you're on the struggle bus and a big gust of wind could blow you away!" Some of you may think I chose some unique words to show my concern, but I was eleven and still had quite a bit to learn about my use of language and delivery.

"Oh, sweetheart I'm fine. It's been a few long weeks and my body is still adjusting." She sweetly changed the subject and told me not to worry.

No matter what she said, I was still worried and continued to press the issue. Eventually, my mom shared she was holding a huge amount of guilt for not being able to uphold the principles of her faith by being divorced.

It wasn't long into our new routine before I noticed my mother was losing weight and appeared more tired than usual. The impact of the change caused her to wonder how much easier things would be in a household with two income earners. While she was thankful for the finances of the shift differential, it took a toll on her body.

She felt she had let God down, disgraced her family, and she worried about the consequences of my father's absence in my life. Not only was I the youngest, but due to the differences in age, my siblings were out of the house, and I was growing up like an only child.

In some respects, the tireless hours my mother spent at work served a penance she was trying to pay. Buying me things was her attempt to make up for the times she struggled to provide for my needs.

It broke my heart to see how the pain and guilt she carried would sometimes influence her life. She wanted to make everyone happy, and this dictated her choices, how she communicated, and the way she pushed herself to succeed. This was further compounded by the oppressive religious dogmas that were a resounding part of her internal narrative.

Growing up she was taught that if a Christian woman leaves their marriage, they have failed. This created a tug of war between the abuse and neglect she endured and her desire to meet the expectations of her family of origin. Deep within her spirit, she found it hard to believe God was not angry she was divorced.

Out of her love for me, she desperately tried to bury her pain and paid a price that never felt like enough.

I have seen multiple versions of these same beliefs and mindsets played out in my work with clients. Whether rooted in faith, a sense of moral standard, or insecurity, people fear judgment more than the pain they endure.

My mother was married for eighteen years before she found the courage and strength to walk away.

It's never too late to make a conscious act of determination.

* * * *

Although I was only eleven, I believed I could bring hope into the pain my mother carried. If she could view her choices without bathing them in judgment, it would quiet her battle with doubt and shame. How did I know this was possible? I grew up watching her encourage others, freely extending a level of grace and support she was unable to give herself.

In ways that most would not recognize, my mother would sometimes shape shift. She would become small in order to help others maintain their sense of superiority. I was hopeful she would come to abandon this response and *fully walk in her power with no regard for those who refused to adjust.*

One winter evening just before dinner, my mother and I were in the groove of our evening routine. Typically, I would wake her up around 6:00 p.m., we would make dinner, and sit together at the table to enjoy our meal. Then we would head to the couch to relax and talk before she left for work.

Earlier in the week, I had taken every possible opportunity to bring up the forbidden topic of her job. It didn't add up in my mind, so I was determined to understand why she would choose to endure such a grueling daily pace. After my last failed attempt, I promised to table the conversation until the weekend.

It was Friday, so now I had the green light. Our bellies were full, and our hearts were open, so I prepared myself to bring up the topic again. After-dinner cleanup seemed like the perfect time. We would be somewhat engaged, so the discussion could stay fairly light.

I smiled, watching my mother scurry around the kitchen, trying not to make eye contact. It was cute but obvious because typically she would be looking at me and dancing around, being silly.

Her avoidance was out of character, but I could tell she sensed a conversation was on the horizon.

Cognizant of what she might have been feeling, I walked over to where she was standing and gently wrapped my arms around her waist. I wanted her to slow down so she could hear the conviction in what I was about to say.

For a few minutes I stood there with the right side of my cheek pressed into her chest, my ear right against her heart. I turned my head and lifted my gaze until our eyes were in sync.

"Mom, you are enough, and you have always been more than enough. I don't need any of the things you're buying, and if I had to choose between all the shopping and you, I would choose you every time."

That was the first time I had seen my mother cry.

I wondered if her tears could speak what they would say. Then again, it didn't really matter. Even if we couldn't put words to everything taking place, something was happening. For me, it was settled; I simply hugged my mother a little tighter and leaned into my own sense of relief and optimism.

We stood there together, tipping the iceberg, and I felt certain of two things:

1. It took a great deal of courage for my mother to let me into her place of pain.
2. Sharing our pain isn't self-pity but helps us feel less alone.

I believe that night was a turning point. My mother later slowed down her daily pace and gave herself permission to rest. Without my prompting, she intentionally shared more of her story, and it helped expand my perspective of her life.

Early in her marriage, several people told her when she learned to meet my father's expectations, he would treat her better. They encouraged her to endure the abuse, like a good wife, and it would eventually go away. This led her to believe anything other than pushing through would be a disgrace to her family and her faith. That advice was not only devastating but left her in constant fear of failing at life.

In the depths of her internal narrative, she had failed in marriage, disappointed her family, and let her children down. Sadly, she spent several years of her life struggling to reconcile these feelings and make up for her mistakes.

Her primary aim was to hide her wounds and at all costs and never fail again. This is an excerpt from one her journal entries written a few months after our night in the kitchen.

When we walk around with invisible wounds, we pay the biggest price. Our presence soon fades, and our voice becomes silent, leaving us seen but not known. The only person I am truly failing is myself.

* * * *

Now, as a mother myself, I have an even greater understanding of the risk and reward of showing vulnerability to our children. As adults, we often want to shield our children from hurt and fear. We believe letting them see our pain will impact their sense of security. Some of us worry our children will view us differently and lose confidence in our strength and ability to care for them.

There is definitely an appropriate balance to consider, and we don't want our children to believe it is their job to fix our problems. However, family is our foundation and where we learn how to manage both the highs and lows of love and life. Moments like my mother and I had in the kitchen helped me broaden my definition of what it meant to be strong—to be a parent.

It taught me strength is a tapestry, created as life takes our most powerful experiences and weaves them in balance with the moments where we feel discouraged, uncertain, or overwhelmed. I absolutely believe fourteen years later when my mother passed away, the vulnerability and transparency she displayed that night was etched into the undercurrent below my iceberg.

When I was tempted to push through and deny my war with grief, I would think back to that night in the kitchen. It reminded me there is power in vulnerability and to never allow the expectations of others to be my guiding light.

Life will tip our iceberg and meeting the expectations of others can no longer be top priority. This may create feelings of guilt or discomfort but making this shift does not mean failure. It *creates a new sense of life balance that doesn't require you to ignore your needs.*

RESTORE:

SAVASANA

Typically, our everyday focus is extended outward. It can be challenging to find consistent time to internally self-reflect. People around us pull on our energy and the day-to-day demands of life can leave us with little time and energy for ourselves.

Savasana is a posture that can become a key ingredient to help us calm down and center. It is often the final posture in yoga but is also a valuable way to engage the mind and body at any time. During Savasana, the boundaries between the mind and body merge. It gives us the opportunity to quiet our inner chatter and internally connect in an adaptive way. If repeatedly practiced, it helps us develop a greater level of awareness and tap into thoughts and feelings that are usually kept under the radar.

Please always remember to take agency as you engage in these mindfulness practices. They are optional and meant to support your work as you engage through this book. For example, if it's uncomfortable to close your eyes, feel free to keep them open. Honor what your mind and body need while working to show gratitude for the courage it takes to show up for yourself.

Lie down on your back. As you recline on a mat or the couch, spread your feet slightly apart from each other. Put your arms at your sides with your palms facing up. Your fingers should curl up naturally.

- Close your eyes and focus on your breathing. Breathe from your diaphragm, which is in your lower belly. Push out the muscles in your diaphragm as you inhale. Inhale for five counts. Then exhale for another five counts.
- Repeat the breathing sequence and work toward allowing your body to release and feel a sense of calm or stillness.

REFLECT:

In moments you find your primary motivation is to meet the standards of others, how does this influence your choices? How about your inner dialogue?

How well are you able to <u>recognize</u> and <u>admit</u> the moments of hurt you've experienced?

If you've ever chosen to hide your discomfort, what made you believe this was the best option?

What would be different if you had a lesser fear of letting yourself down?

RECALIBRATE:

The Mindset: When I don't live up to what people expect, I feel like I've failed

*Use the space below to develop a **mental shift** statement to help recalibrate your perspective on the mindset above:*

Seeing Beyond
the Known

---

*The Mindset: Life has taught me what to
expect; why set myself up believing for more?*

When people come to my office, there are numerous explanations for the mindsets that dictate their lives. One of the most common beliefs I hear is, "I have always been this way" or "I am just like my mom or dad." Some feel overwhelmed and the root of their mindset is to do whatever it takes to avoid conflict.

Then there are clients who have spent so much time pleasing others, they've lost sight of what they believe or who they are outside of obedience. They mimic their environments and the thought of breaking away from this pattern is terrifying.

Have you ever heard someone mention they are exhausted, but you could tell they meant more than just physically? I have often found people acknowledge a lack of emotional energy but focusing on their needs is a struggle. Constant disappointment and feeling devalued has led them to believe they're the only person they can trust. From their perspective, life never works according to plan, and in the rare moment it looks promising, an issue is bound to arise. Over time, these conclusions can take over and influence every aspect of their lives.

Unhealthy primary mindsets can cause us to invest significant effort in creating what I call *beautiful chaos*, while desperately seeking a way to heal in secret. *Beautiful chaos* is created when we work to present our life as always wonderful and filled with gratitude, only leaving room to address the positive emotions. The goal is to make life appear so wonderful that no one will see a glimpse of what's crumbling underneath.

The opposite of beautiful chaos is *rigid mindsets*, built solely upon logic and order. Emotions are considered problematic and seen as barriers to choices that should be black and white. Mindsets like toxic positivity and rigidity are representative of beliefs that fall along a continuum of control and create collateral damage.

Control is an overestimation of our ability to make things go the way we desire. It is often founded in emotions such as fear, insecurity, entitlement, and privilege. Control seeking mindsets disregard how getting what we want impacts the other people in our lives.

Operating from a place of our highest potential does not mean we will always feel in control. Our potential thrives when we understand our sense of confidence and security isn't healthy when attached to outcomes. It rests in the power of our perspective.

The automatic patterns that emerge when things don't go our way will show us which mindsets are in charge. For example, when we apply for jobs, we have no control over the outcome. We can create a resumé and be selected for interviews, but consistently be denied an opportunity. If we become overly attached to the outcome, we will take the denials personally, view them as rejection, and immediately begin to doubt our abilities.

Operating from a perspective of potential will encourage you to learn from the process and to be curious about how you can improve your ability to translate and attract the opportunities you want. Most of all, a perspective of potential will allow you to move forward in confidence, believing the right timing and the right door will eventually align.

* * * *

Our relationships, especially those that require vulnerability, also help illuminate the primary mindsets at play.

My husband Randy and I were married a few weeks after I turned twenty-two. Although I was excited, this was not part of my original plan. Heading into college, I was focused on my career and dating was not a priority.

When my sisters encouraged me to keep my options open and seize the moment, I would smile and laugh returning my attention back to my own plan. *Enjoy college, focus on my career plans, and have a little fun on the side.*

I made it through the first year of college without dating, and thought to myself, why abandon that now. Then life so eloquently changed and reminded me to "sit down and have several seats!"

Early into my sophomore year, a fiery and handsome young man came into my life and eventually took my heart by surprise. Remember who I was at that time. This wasn't love at first sight.

We both showed an initial air of arrogance and intentionally ignored each other, even when our social circles crossed paths.

Without our knowledge, one of our mutual friends, Evie, was plotting our paths to cross. Whether she saw something that made her believe we were a good fit, or she was having fun at our expense, it worked.

The first time Randy and I spoke, the conversation felt like home. We were there in Evie's apartment, sitting at the edge of the hallway, facing one another with our backs leaned against the wall. There were no butterflies in my stomach or awkward moments of small talk, which was a win in my book.

In between sharing my strong opinions and a laundry list of what I didn't tolerate in friends, Randy made me laugh like no one else could. He wasn't necessarily trying to be funny, but he was so quick-witted and direct with his assumptions that it was exciting to see what he'd say next.

That night we exchanged numbers and kept talking until we realized that some amount of sleep was necessary to survive class the next day.

Randy and I enjoyed the early months of our friendship, which eliminated any pressure to perform. I never felt the need to become a version of myself based on his preferences. Our relationship was naturally taking a cadence of its own.

As our love began to form, the relationship remained steady and transparent, which was a true source of comfort. I have never been one for games, so there was a great sense of security in knowing where things stood...or so I thought.

* * * *

As time went along, Randy and I settled into navigating the demands of college, working part-time, and keeping up with all the other responsibilities in our lives. The days were filled with making memories, singing together in choir, and hysterical laughter. He was becoming a trusted friend.

True to any healthy relationship, there were also challenging moments. Some of my perspectives were quite rigid, and while I knew they sometimes created friction, I was determined to hold my ground.

When I was upset, I would become quiet and isolate. This was one of the primary ways I managed the distance between the intensity of my emotions. It had proven to be a better alternative than my natural habit of using sharp words to put people in place.

Randy wasn't in favor of this approach, and his way of dealing with conflict placed us on opposite sides of the fence. He was unafraid of my emotional intensity and preferred to stay in the discomfort and talk it out.

From my perspective, there was nothing about his perspective that seemed valuable. I was not only convinced my way was right, but it also struck a nerve to feel like "some man" was trying to tell me what to do.

Growing up in a home without a constant male presence left me with little knowledge of partner communication. There may be some of you who grew up with a father and can equally relate, but there are some unique views and survival skills that develop when raised by a single parent. It can require or suggest adopting a level of self-sufficiency that excludes the need to rely on or trust in anyone other than yourself.

In my case, the absence of my father created a pervasive assumption that men could not be trusted with my heart.

It was more comfortable to internalize my emotions and remain quiet until I was ready to talk. This process kept me out of trouble in school, allowed my mother to breathe a little easier (not bracing for my brutal honesty), and taught me the art of intentional word choice. This had proven to be an effective source of strength, but not in my relationship with Randy. When I couldn't rely on this pattern, even small moments of disagreement felt threatening. I could feel any hint of conflict surging through my body, which always led to the same conclusion.

He is going to leave!

In my heart, I was convincing myself Randy would soon decide I wasn't worth keeping around. This was such an odd thought because there was also a part of me that felt confident in who I was and what I brought into his life. The first few times I had these thoughts, they were easily dismissed. I chalked it up to the dynamics of young love and a new relationship.

Eventually, this mindset became more difficult to overlook. The undercurrent of my fear grew louder and more frequent, until one evening I could no longer quiet it down.

We were sitting in the car, just before our 1:00 a.m. curfew, enjoying the final moments before heading into our dorms. The spring weather was mild, and the windows were slightly cracked, letting in the faint sound of the buzzing street lights just behind the car. That night we turned off the music and seemed to simultaneously listen for who would be the first to speak.

Randy turned in my direction, gently placed his hands on my cheeks and patiently waited for my gaze to lock with his. Then he calmly said, "I'm not going anywhere. Even if we disagree, I will never leave you." Time felt like it was standing still and waiting for me to give it permission to continue.

I wanted to let Randy's words sink deep into my being, but instead I felt frozen. My mouth was as pasty and dry as a desert, and my normal quick wit was nowhere to be found. Randy always had a way of seeing past my defenses, but this felt next level. He hit on a nerve I was still trying to figure out and the only response I could think to say was, "thank you."

On my drive home I had a talk with myself, "Really Charryse, thank you? That doesn't even make sense. You are losing your edge." I walked into my apartment and collapsed on the couch, while my mind replayed Randy's words like a song on repeat.

* * * *

A piece of my iceberg was beginning to melt, yielding to a change of state due to Randy's warmth. You learn so much about yourself when feelings you've tried to avoid erupt like a geyser.

A few days later, I was able to connect the dots. My fear around Randy leaving was directly connected to the unresolved hurt from my father's absence. The pain had always been there but remained dormant until Randy's love caused it to be exposed.

There are certain mindsets that require a relationship to be revealed and have an opportunity to heal. When we are intimately connected with the right kind of person, they will not enable your avoidance, but they will guard and protect your pain.

The nature of their temperament and values will hold appropriate space as you work to heal. They will see past your resistance and need for control and recognize it's a shield you've learned to carry. Unafraid of your pain, they will choose to stay close, even when fear may be tempting you to pull away.

The steadiness of their love can dare you to believe, and you will realize it may be okay to let your guard down.

It was never Randy's responsibility to mend my brokenness. Expecting this would have been selfish and unrealistic, and undoubtedly set him up for failure. I had to make a decision that learning to trust and receive love was worth the risk. It was a repeated process of learning to look beyond the surface and see through my own roadblocks.

Healing is continuous work that doesn't always involve a target or destination. It's a process of learning and unlearning as we move through the context of our lives. Holding space for self-examination allows us to be curious about the nature of our thoughts and habits. We learn it's not about immediately relieving our emotional pain but staying open and honest about our motivations.

Each time I asked Randy, "Are you going to leave?" it was a test of trust.

My motivation was to protect myself and stay ahead of disappointment. Operating from this mindset limited my field of vision and overlooked how this questioning made him feel. I learned to accept my feelings of hurt and abandonment, while wondering why I didn't notice them before. I thought my father's rejection came so early, leaving me untouched, but clearly, I was very wrong.

About two years after that night, we met in the hallway, Randy and I were married and other areas in need of healing continued to unfold.

Each new situation or stressor required me to adjust the *work* that was already in place. My communication patterns were more flexible, but inevitably something would happen, and I was tempted to go back into my shell. We were well into our fifth year of marriage, before the feelings of abandonment were no longer an automatic default for me.

Many mindsets take time and persistence before they will be fully uprooted. Life can feel like a sitcom, but our issues will not be solved in thirty minutes or less.

* * * *

Resistance can run parallel to the new layers of vulnerability that become unearthed. It can make us point fingers in the wrong direction and show unwillingness to own our part. Resistance to addressing our emotions can create confusion and make us difficult to please.

I also needed to work on asking for support. My needs would vacillate, and this would sometimes make our relationship feel like a game of chess. When I felt uncertain, my need for closeness and reassurance increased. But when I returned to a place of confidence, I wanted space and independence.

Much like resistance, uncertainty can tempt us to find comfort in surrounding ourselves with people who won't challenge the habits we want to maintain. This can occur when we focus on the needs of others at the expense of our own. We may even convince ourselves pulling back and making our needs a priority could be detrimental to those we love. Moreover, living from this mindset can create a circle of self-serving friendships that take more than they give. These "friends" are like leeches who suck you dry and roll away once they're done.

* * * *

Life experiences will undoubtedly influence our expectations, but we must be careful not to believe they are conclusive of our future. When we attempt to move forward while carrying the weight of our past, everyone in our path pays the price. Unresolved hurt can keep us in a loop of trauma that widens the space between today's hurt and tomorrow's healing.

When we walk, the use of our vision is an instinctive process we often overlook. Our sight confirms what's ahead and signals our mind to take the next step. Healing works in a similar fashion, but sometimes we won't have all the answers. We must look beyond the known and have faith in possibility. The ability to see, both literally and figuratively, is one of life's greatest privileges.

My encounter with Greg has always added meaning to this belief.

He and I met one summer while I was traveling in New Mexico. We were walking along a trail and he and his then fiancée stopped to take in the view. In this part of the country, the land is flat, and the sky is so close you feel as if you can reach up and grab the clouds with your hands.

It was a warm and clear night, just before sunset, and the sky was painted in beautiful hues of blue, yellow, pink, and orange.

It was one of those moments where you had to stop and take it all in because even a picture would not do it justice.

As our small caravan of travelers stopped to embrace the moment, Greg's fiancée Jill handed him a gift. Greg carefully opened the small gift bag and took out a pair of special sunglasses. Jill turned toward us long enough to share that Greg was colorblind and for his birthday today she wanted to give him the gift of seeing his first sunset. Greg held the glasses in his hand, inspected them, and with a look of hesitation slowly secured them onto his face.

Within seconds, Greg bent over with his hands placed on his knees, weeping as he looked out toward the sky. Still catching his breath, he stood up tall and slowly began to look from side to side, taking in all that was around him. Then he proclaimed, "This is incredible! Is this what I have been missing all this time?"

Up until that point, Greg had the ability to look, but he was unable to truly see. He was skeptical the glasses would work and told us he often thought other people were being dramatic about the difference. *He had become so conditioned to seeing life as it was, his mind could not picture what was possible.*

Vulnerability helps ignite the courage we need to intentionally move forward. It is an opportunity to use the process of self-discovery to realign the vision we have of ourselves.

Better is possible.

RESTORE:

PURSED LIP BREATHING

This simple breathing technique makes you slow down your pace of breathing by having you apply deliberate effort in each breath.

You can practice at any time...

Practice using this breath four to five times a day when you begin to correctly learn the breathing pattern.

To do it:

1. Relax your neck and shoulders.
2. Keeping your mouth closed, inhale slowly through your nose for two counts.
3. Pucker or purse your lips as though you were going to whistle.
4. Exhale slowly by blowing air through your pursed lips for a count of four.

REFLECT:

How would you describe the difference between looking and seeing? Think about this in the context of stepping back and observing yourself.

In what areas of life do you resist growth, perhaps by repeating patterns that lead you back to the start?

What have you noticed about the people around you that is difficult to see?

How do things play out in the moments you put pressure on yourself to move quickly through unwanted experiences?

RECALIBRATE:

The Mindset: Life has taught me what to expect; why set myself up believing for more?

*Use the space below to develop a **mental shift** to help recalibrate your perspective on the mindset above:*

It's NOT Too Late

———

The Mindset: I've always been this way; I feel like change is impossible.

Let's take a moment to pause and check in. What do you notice as you read through these pages? What thoughts or emotions have come to the surface? Are you allowing yourself to think without filtering? Do you notice the areas of your body that respond when something strikes a chord?

In your day-to-day life, you may go through the motions, but I invite you again to take off your mask.

This means allowing yourself to look beneath what you show to the world and being honest about the parts of yourself that may be hiding underneath. There is so much power and brilliance in the collective stories you have to tell. Separating yourself from the full essence of your experiences is like considering a puzzle complete when there are missing pieces.

Remember, this book isn't meant for you to breeze through and check off your must-read list. It is designed to be read, felt, and moved through at a pace that honors your life's rhythm.

The personal stories I have shared were meant to delay your participation in immediate vulnerability. My hope is you're making parallels pertinent to your life. To grasp the benefits of this process, your vulnerability and buy-in is required.

This is about you.

This is *not* about what others think of you.

This is *not* about getting to the end of this book and having all the answers.

It is your opportunity to dive into the depths of your own iceberg. To help you navigate these waters, I want to bring in some very basic elements of neuroscience.

What is neuroscience? I'm so glad you asked! It focuses on the brain and how it impacts our thoughts and behaviors in connection to our nervous system (Sapolsky 2017).

If this is new information and completely unfamiliar territory, I promise to keep it as simple, and don't worry, there won't be a quiz at the end of the chapter. I believe this knowledge is foundational to grasping your innate power and ability to **rewire and rewrite the narrative you are currently living out**.

Keep an open mind and if you feel overwhelmed, slow down and reread this chapter. You might even surprise yourself, become curious, and want to explore other resources on the topic.

* * * *

When the struggles in our lives play on repeat, our individual responses will be unique. Sometimes we can take it all in stride and be patient with our process of repair. Other times challenges catch us off guard, and we may become frustrated and believe our past efforts weren't a true sign of growth. There may also be instances when we only address our struggles on the surface, enough to soften the initial blow. *We've diminished the true impact of our past or even allowed others to convince us our felt experiences are not a big deal.* If we are not careful, blunting our feelings can become a habit.

Here are some other reasons we avoid our emotions:

- Desire to compartmentalize the event.
- Belief the situation would create disappointment.
- Staying quiet creates feelings of control.
- Past traumatic experiences have minimized the impact.
- Concerned other emotions may surface.

Sometimes we believe reconciling the past can feel like betrayal. It can feel like breaking a secret silence we've been taught to maintain. This is a common sentiment expressed by my clients and something I have noticed in my own life.

There weren't any direct encounters that led me to hide the recall of my sexual abuse, but rather reinforced implicit messages—silence was best.

Growing up in church, anything regarding the body was communicated through a lens of shame. Conversations were often limited to sex before marriage and purity culture didn't tell you how to heal when your purity was taken away.

Early experiences of stigma and family judgment were still freshly imprinted in my brain. Opening up would have felt like providing the prosecution with evidence to mark my life *destined for dysfunction.*

I had also accumulated certain perceptions toward cultural norms and disclosure. The Black culture has a long-standing value of *what happens in this house, stays in the house.* Resiliency in my house meant keeping things under wrap and limiting the amount of time and energy spent addressing challenges.

The thought of adding to my mother's emotional burden also made me cautious. She was finally in a place where her life was settling down and giving her room to heal.

So, when my repressed memories surfaced, I decided *my work* was to find the balance between processing the situation, protecting those I loved, and not holding myself captive.

Making peace with our past is a restorative process. When we give our mental load permission to lighten—to operate through honesty and transparency—we open the pathway for change.

* * * *

The principles of neuroscience show us the human brain is wired for survival.

In the early 1900s, the "father of neuroscience," Santiago Ramón y Cajal, talked about "neuronal plasticity." He recognized, in contrast to the current belief at that time, brains could indeed change after adulthood was reached (Fuchs and Flugge 2014).

Neurons in the brain are built like trees with branches that come out of each cell and run along the systems of the body. Together they form neural pathways that group together based on our frequent habits, thoughts, and behaviors (Sapolsky 2017).

Neurons in our brain connect to every system of our body. We will circle back to this later, but this means our thoughts absolutely impact our physical well-being. Optimally, our mental health and physical health are designed to work together.

The health of our brain's pathways is directly related to our *frequent habits. Our everyday patterns significantly influence what we believe and how we feel.* They will either move us in the direction of ease or the direction of dis-ease.

This principle is reflected by the phrase, "Neurons that fire together, wire together," coined by Canadian neuropsychologist Donald Hebb. Repeated experiences activate and strengthen our brain's neurons, creating automatic patterns. When those patterns are healthy and flexible, it's beneficial (Van Der Kolk 2014).

Moving toward a direction of ease means living in a way that honors the life we desire, while maintaining a general sense of well-being.

It does not mean our lives are perfect, but there is clarity and intentional effort toward navigating life with flexibility. When experiences can be viewed through multiple perspectives, it increases our ability to use our wise mind. Developed by psychologist Marcia Linehan, conceptually, the wise mind uses a balance of both logic and emotions to engage in analysis (Sturgeon 2020).

In contrast, moving in the direction of dis-ease is like trying to find a lost car at the airport. Every time we think we're walking a different way we end up where we started.

This leaves us feeling stuck and wondering if it's worth the effort to keep trying. Everything feels like a challenge or a battle we try to fight with a mind and body that has already been bruised and battered. A dead end feels inevitable and giving up may feel like the best option.

This outlook reminds me of sentiments expressed by Donovan, a client I supported in the early years of my counseling career.

* * * *

Donovan walked through my door as a twenty-eight-year-old business professional. He immediately shared it had taken him several months to work up the courage to call and follow through with an appointment. He felt seeking support through therapy was a condition of poor self-will and discipline.

As a result of this belief, much of his mental energy was spent battling feelings of failure and shame.

By all accounts, Donovan was considered highly successful. He had completed both his bachelor's and master's degrees, graduated with honors, and moved directly into a full-time role with a large local industry. Within the last two years he had created a successful nonprofit with strong financial backing that centered around his areas of passion. This was the perfect balance to the well-paying job he found mundane and unfulfilling.

In Donovan's mind, he was doing what was expected and living a life that would make most people proud.

He also had great friends and a strong relationship with his family. Donovan knew he was embedded in a loving and supportive community that was always there to help. Yet, he battled constant anxiety that would significantly increase when making any kind of decision. He was doing all the right things but wondered why he still felt afraid.

By the time our first session ended, Donovan appeared more comfortable and expressed interest in further exploring the issues we discussed that day. He acknowledged a sense of relief in being honest about his struggles. At one point he said, "I wish I would have taken this step sooner."

An appointment was scheduled for the following week, but he didn't show up.

About a month later, he sent an email acknowledging his doubt. He wrote, "I am so afraid that changing the way I feel won't work. Is it even possible after all this time? I don't want to waste your time and take up the space you could be using to help people with bigger problems."

It always breaks my heart when someone feels reaching for support would be a waste of time or a burden, but it is a very common underlying belief.

There can be a strong degree of uncertainty when we reach out for help. According to neuroscience, the brain registers uncertainty like an error, which creates a fear of failure and a desire to stay safe through avoidance (Anderson et al. 2019).

You are not a burden.
You are worth the time and effort.
You already possess the answers you seek.

I can say these statements and dozens more with similar themes, but it will come down to what you believe. What do you believe about yourself and how you are walking through life right now? What has been the cost of the mindsets you hide from others but constantly battle?

The points of pain you carry are not a sign of weakness and regardless of the part you have played, eternal punishment will not bring relief.

* * * *

Leslie was in her midforties and began restricting her food when she was a freshman in college. She always thought it was a behavior she could stop, but almost twenty-five years later her eating disorder was worse than ever.

When we met, it was the first time she had been completely honest about the details of her eating habits.

She said, "This is my fault, I knew what I was doing when I started restricting my calories, so how can I ask for help when I've done this to myself?"

As I connected with Leslie and began learning about her life, she revealed more layers of her story.

Leading up to college, her life was marked by economic instability, parental abandonment, and bullying. These challenges weren't left behind when she went to college. They collided with the demands of this significant life change.

We risk adopting an unbalanced version of the truth when we solely blame our choices, instead of examining the context of our experiences.

The transition to adulthood that occurs when entering college is one of the top ten stressors experienced in life (Pedrelli et al. 2015). This can be further complicated by any traumas or stressors experienced in childhood, adolescence, or during the teen years.

In a subsequent session, Leslie admitted she almost didn't return to therapy. Every week for the first three months she expressed her doubt and asked for reassurance that she was not wasting my time—that her situation was not hopeless. She also voiced uncertainty about letting her guard down and trusting I wasn't simply consoling her broken spirit.

One of my initial goals with Leslie was to help her understand how her emotions, her brain, and her body were connected.

We began with small doses of neuroscience much like we discussed earlier, but in greater detail. I wanted her to have some basic education on the principles we would use. Finding out her situation was rooted in science built her trust and decreased her concerns I was only doing my job and saying what she wanted to hear.

I am passionate about my role as a therapist and have enough optimism for us all but hope and belief in your healing is also *founded on solid research and study.* When it comes to how our brain supports our growth, knowledge is power.

There are universal aspects to how our brain functions. If you were born with a full spectrum of brain functioning, you possess the potential to supersede your experiences (Leaf 2013).

You can overcome the choices you have made and the choices that have been forced upon you. Our brains specialize in exceeding our expectations!

* * * *

The human brain has one hundred billion neurons that form about one thousand connections to other neurons. One of its most unique aspects is the ability to regenerate. Think of it as having special powers to come back to life (Barlow, Durand, and Hofmann, 2018).

Neural pathways darken like leaves on a rotting tree when damaged by negative thinking, long-term emotional challenges, or even a toxic living environment (Leaf 2013).

If this happens, it is not the end of the road. The neural networks in our brain *can change* through growth and reorganization (Stiles and Jernigan 2010).

Dr. Celeste Campbell is a neuropsychologist who has completed extensive research and worked with individuals across the developmental life span. Her summation of neuroplasticity highlights some important aspects that can transform what you believe is possible.

Dr. Campbell states, *"Neuroplasticity refers to the brain's ability to adapt. It refers to the physiological changes in the brain that happen as the result of our interactions with our environment. From the time the brain begins to develop in utero until the day we die, the connections among the cells in our brains reorganize in response to our changing needs. This dynamic process allows us to learn from and adapt to different experiences"* (2016).

When we engage in activities such as learning a new skill, making a positive change in our environment, or even increasing our sleep, it creates the fuel our brain needs to begin shifting (Leaf 2013). Tasks, such as these, reinforce our understanding and ability to find hope in neuroplasticity and the brain's ability to make new connections.

* * * *

In many ways, infants provide some amazing examples of how to move through an experience without letting it highjack the mindset.

Have you ever heard of the 90 Second Emotion Rule? This concept was developed by Harvard scientist Dr. Jill Bolte Taylor as she used her knowledge of neuroscience to better understand her own experiences after suffering a stroke (Taylor 2008).

Strong emotions create a chemical process that only takes ninety seconds to initiate, surge through the bloodstream, and get flushed out (Taylor 2008).

Our automatic response ends, and our ongoing emotional reactions are a result of *the stories we create and choose to replay in our minds* (Taylor 2008).

Collectively, the intensity of this process depends on the biological, psychological, and social factors each person has experienced (Leaf 2013).

Biological factors include areas such as age, gender, and genetic predisposition. Psychological factors involve variables such as coping skills, past trauma experiences, and level of emotional distress. Social factors involve the influence of our support system, cultural factors, and the quality of interpersonal relationships (Barlow, Durand, and Hofmann 2018).

When my daughter Cierra was six weeks old, we took her to get her ears pierced. Yes, I am that mom and have no shame!

Some people thought I was crazy but there was a reason I chose to get this done so early. I knew she would not remember the pain.

When we went inside the jewelry store, she was sleeping. The tech prepped her ears and proceeded to pierce them one at a time.

She cried for about thirty to forty-five seconds after each ear was pierced. Talk about the 90 Second Rule in action!

Yes, she felt a tinge of pain through her body, and it startled her, but those physical reactions quickly went away.

I am happy to report she then went on with her life, and other than what we've told her, she doesn't remember a thing.

If we would have waited until she was eight years old, the experience would have been much more intense. She would have direct memory of every step of the process and even have a string of thoughts around what piercing would be like.

In both scenarios, the true level of pain would be the same, but as an anxious adolescent child, her narrative around the experience would be on loop and constantly create fear. That same fear would then activate every time she anticipated an unknown situation.

What I want you to grasp is both the actual experience and what you tell yourself about that experience maintain the emotions around the situation. When we replay the worst-case scenarios or view them through a distorted perspective, we can feel trapped and carry these messages into every area of our lives.

Understanding the infinite capacity you have for growth can be powerful and transformative at any stage of life. Whether personally or professionally, complacency comes at a cost you don't have to pay. There is room in every story for a better ending.

It is not too late.

RESTORE:

Please always remember to take agency as you engage in these mindfulness practices. They are optional and meant to support your work as you engage through this book. Honor what your mind and body need, while working to show gratitude for the courage it takes to show up for yourself. It is best to read through this exercise and then begin. Start off aiming for three minutes, and as you practice, work your way up to ten to fifteen minutes. This is an optional range, not a goal. Trust yourself to know when to begin and end. You decide.

OBSERVE YOUR OWN THOUGHTS

In the moments we are aware of our thoughts, they can feel like they are all coming at one time. If these thoughts are perceived as a threat, we will distract and avoid, doing whatever we can to tell ourselves we don't have time. I want to invite you to practice this mindfulness exercise designed to enhance your awareness of your thoughts.

To begin, sit or lie down in any position you find comfortable. Then try and let all the tension in your body slowly begin to release. This is harder than it sounds, so extend yourself some grace. Scan your body from the top of your head and travel down toward your feet, noticing where there is room for you to let go of where you're holding on.

Begin to focus on your breathing first, then move your awareness to the inside of your body. Notice what it is like to live inside your body. If any emotion comes up here, see what it would be like not to push it away. Then turn your attention toward your thoughts.

Be aware of what comes into your mind but challenge the urge to label or judge these thoughts. Think of them as a passing cloud in the sky and remind yourself these thoughts in and of themselves cannot diminish your power unless you let them. They are just thoughts.

If your mind wanders notice it, focus on your breath, and then guide yourself back to this practice.

Optional: Engage in this exercise while listening to binaural beats through headphones. Binaural beats combine the knowledge of neuroscience (science of the brain) and sound frequency to strengthen connections within your brain.

*Binaural beats can be accessed for free on music platforms such as Spotify, Apple Music, Pandora, or Amazon Music.

REFLECT:

What are your biggest takeaways from this chapter? How do they personally relate to your life?

What have you been telling yourself about your ability to move through your mental roadblocks? Your mental roadblocks are the thoughts and emotions that surface when you are outside of your comfort zone.

Can you identify any **specific beliefs** about yourself or your abilities that hurt your mental and/or physical well-being?

How do you think your current environment would respond or support your efforts toward personal growth?

Describe any ways your current environment may be holding you back.

RECALIBRATE:

The Mindset: This is the way I have always been; I don't think it will change.

*Use the space below to develop a **mental shift** statement to help recalibrate your perspective on the mindset above:*

System Updates Available

———

The Mindset: I should be able to overcome my challenges on my own.

In this day and age so much of our daily productivity centers around technology. Everywhere we go there's a charging station. They're strategically located all throughout our homes, our cars, the airports, and restaurants. You can even purchase cordless and battery-operated charging units.

Most of us keep a careful eye on the battery life of the devices we use and quickly respond when we notice a system update is available.

Updates ensure our devices utilize the best available version of operating software. If we ignore or delay the reminders for these updates the device's system slows down, and there are issues with overall performance, which can cause the system as a whole to crash.

Updates are critical and contain bugs and fixes that repair and maintain the system's overall functioning. They also reinforce safety and reduce vulnerabilities that would make the system prone to viruses or data loss.

We can use this analogy to view ourselves through a similar lens and optimize our own operating system.

The mind, body, and spirit collectively make up the human system, and they are designed to work in holistic harmony. As individuals, we frequently struggle because we often band-aid symptoms instead of addressing our challenges through a comprehensive lens.

When feelings such as anxiety, anger, impulsivity, and irritability arise, we often diminish or rationalize their presence instead of exploring the root of their origin.

Trying to manage symptoms alone is much like playing an old arcade game called whack-a-mole. In this game you grab a mallet and see if you can pop a mole on the head, forcing it back into its hole. It may sound easy, but as soon as you hit one mole, another one immediately rears its head.

As you play the game, the moles pop up faster and faster. Before long, you are hysterically laughing and a bit exhausted from trying to keep them all down at the same time.

Some of us walk around playing the same game with our health and well-being. Outwardly, we seem fine, but inside we are like zombies walking through the day trying to avoid the emotional land mines that may fire off at any moment.

During Elena's first visit to my office, she was very clear her desire was to focus on the specialized support I offer for eating disorders.

She was working with another therapist and did not feel their work adequately addressed this area. I immediately educated Elena on the mind-gut connection and the ways in which disordered eating symptoms are directly connected to our emotions.

Whether someone restricts themselves by eating less food than their body needs or binging by eating more than their body can safely consume at one time, the underlying motives can be similar (Mehler and Andersen 2017).

There is often a desire to use food as a means of avoidance or to control the intensity of other emotions that feel overwhelming.

We all have conscious and unconscious thoughts about food and eating (Grilo and Mitchell 2010). Exploration of how we engage with food beyond biological necessity can hold discoverable meaning toward our emotional well-being. Food may be used to:

- exercise a sense of control and autonomy.
- create feelings of superiority through adherence to food rules and restriction.
- numb out and disconnect from situations outside of our control.
- self-soothe and provide comfort when feeling emotions such as stress, anxiety, or sadness.

Early in our session, Elena admitted she was fairly stubborn. It was as if she was trying to warn me she could be a threat.

I smiled and said, *"Persistence when channeled in the right direction can be powerful but being stubborn at your own expense is like seeing your exit and choosing to drive in circles while being frustrated you're lost."*

Elena wanted to immediately work on modifying her behaviors without ***exploring the underlying emotions*** but honoring this desire would have thrust her into a real-life game of whack-a-mole.

Healing from our maladaptive coping patterns <u>is not a matter of getting great advice or a series of steps to follow</u>. We must work to develop a depth of personal insight that sheds light on:

- what our coping patterns reveal about our mindset,
- how our patterns have developed over time, and
- why we maintain patterns that provide short-term relief followed by long-term consequences.

In Elena's mind, being stubborn meant *resistance to change.*

She was afraid shifting her beliefs around her relationship with food would require her to change her identity and her convictions and abandon the habits she had always known.

Elena, like many, wanted to maintain what she considered the best of both worlds.

She wanted to feel better while holding on to the outdated messages and belief systems fueling her struggles. In her mind, minimizing the magnitude of her eating disorder would make it simple to overcome and protect the view she had of herself.

Admit when there are issues.

* * * *

The first two weeks Elena seemed motivated despite achieving what she considered minimal success.

We spent time exploring her current relationship around food as well as the emotions that surfaced during food experiences, she found overwhelming. In Elena's case, making decisions around what to eat and preparing meals was challenging. As a result, she would delay her meals and experience intense hunger cues around mid-afternoon.

This would lead her to eating more than she felt comfortable eating and at times led to physical discomfort. She would then go to bed filled with guilt and a sense of defeat as well as planning how to restrict and compensate the next day.

This is an endless cycle that left her fighting against their emotions and biological needs for nourishment and energy.

Together, Elena and I identified meals that organically fit into her comfort zone, and she established goals around eating at set meal times. Her desire was to create more consistency and structure within her day and decrease her restrictive eating patterns.

We also set goals around tracking and noticing her internal experiences before, during, and after meals.

Elena was **resistant to believing her emotions played such a primary role** in how she engaged with food. In her mind, it was a matter of discipline and being too picky, therefore, limiting her food options.

In my work with clients, this can be a common stance regarding recurring habits. Focusing solely on the behavior is often an effort to minimize its magnitude and convince ourselves it's a simple fix. Any behavior that's difficult to change has an emotional undercurrent running the show.

After the third week of these efforts, Elena tearfully entered the session and remarked, "I am not doing well in any area, and I don't understand why I can't move past this point."

She had focused all her strength on modifying her eating patterns but found herself in a place where other challenges had intensified.

Her anxiety was through the roof, she had very little motivation, and despite trying to reduce her alcohol consumption, she was drinking three to four times daily.

Elena was losing at her unintentional game of mental whack-a-mole and felt ashamed and disappointed the game couldn't be won through grit and will. She slowly began to recognize she could not choose to "fix" one issue at a time while ignoring its influence on every other area of her life.

Her stubbornness was the evil twin to perseverance and her unwavering allegiance to this mindset caused her system to crash.

Thankfully, this experience pushed Elena to a place where she became open to updating her beliefs. She recognized *her way of navigating life was outdated and the motivation behind holding her ground was getting in her way.* This was not the first time her system experienced a crash, but the pattern of poor performance was now rapidly cycling back, eliminating her attempts to negotiate.

Elena had a habit of convincing herself if her mental well-being did not leave her in a state of extreme discomfort, she was overreacting and being dramatic. Elena did not understand the consequence of what she was telling herself or even realize the damage of invalidating her struggles.

Seek to understand.

In order to release what no longer serves us and activate our highest potential, we must understand and then update how we use our mind. Our minds are like the software of our system; it is the component that tells our hardware, our body and spirit, how to function and make choices.

Digital devices have unique operating systems specific to their design. As individuals we function in a similar fashion. Even when similarities exist, *what works for one person may not work for another.*

Your personal algorithm informs the way you solve problems and how you translate the process into different situations. This is a simple adaptation of how I teach this concept to my clients.

Personal Algorithm Process (PAP)

- Step 1 – Identify the facts (not assumptions) around the problem.
- Step 2 – Analyze your beliefs toward the situation and your ability to manage it successfully.
- Step 3 – Determine what skills or support you need to actively work on a solution. Are they available?
- Step 4 – Examine your response to the situation and what it reveals about how you cope.
- Step 5 – Revise your plan and make any adjustments that improve your ability to function.

When we look to others to tell us who we are, what we should believe, and how we should operate, it can lead to confusion. It can also leave us feeling disappointed when we yield different results.

I may emphasize this a million more times but understanding yourself is a titrated process. This means *you will need to continuously measure, adjust, and balance everything you may need to operate as the best version of yourself.*

During our ongoing work, Elena would often refer to her identity during college. Based on what she shared, this season of life was not a walk in the park, but it was the last time her system did not seem so significantly offline.

She came to realize most of her current challenges were also present during that season of life. The only difference was the pace of life in college provided her with constant opportunities to use distraction as a way to cope.

Elena, now removed from that season, was able to look back and view it from another perspective. She took as many classes as possible, constantly volunteered for key roles in clubs and organizations, worked more than needed, and ate as little as possible while exercising six days a week.

"Everyone around me thought I had it all together, but I was constantly drinking and felt just as anxious and afraid as I do now." Being busy was Elena's way of minimizing her problems and hiding them from others.

While we can have a semblance of understanding when in the midst of a challenging season, there will also be elements of emotional resistance that will block our full degree of understanding. It often requires us to get through a situation, catch our breath, and then look back before we can learn to see the experience as an observer versus a survivor.

When we shift into being an observer we notice the quality of our thoughts, subtle emotions, and behaviors. We examine our mindsets with an *openness to truth* and view our past experiences through a nonjudgmental lens.

Know your vulnerabilities.

* * *

Prior to reaching out, Elena was unfulfilled and lacked direction.

She woke up every day, ate breakfast, walked the dogs, and had only a few hours of work to keep her busy. Over the course of our work together, she realized having too much idle time on her hands was a significant risk factor, making her vulnerable to self-medicating.

She would self–medicate through actions such as controlling her food choices, obsessively working to change her body, or looking for the next big achievement that could serve as a means of mental distraction.

When these actions did not work, Elena would become anxious and depressed, then quietly retreat to her room, and drink herself to sleep for the night. To add context, this occurred while living with her parents and siblings. Everyone was off doing their own thing and chalked up her isolation to a young adult's need for space.

Following graduation, Elena moved home where she lacked connection and community. She felt socially awkward and anxious when interacting with people she didn't know well. The college atmosphere was like forced exposure therapy, pushing her to engage with others and develop a sense of connection. Yet, as soon as she left school, so did her desire to push past her social anxiety and work to build new community.

Working from home did not provide Elena with a chance to connect with her coworkers or be invited out. She seamlessly retreated to her natural default patterns, but there was a problem. Her core patterns of avoidance and isolation didn't work as she expected. Being by herself was painful and left her vulnerable to feelings of hopelessness and depression. She would lose hours of her day caught in a spiral of negative thoughts.

We would like to think something like this could never happen in our home, but challenges such as depression affect people from every facet of life. According to the latest research by the National Alliance on Mental Illness (NAMI) 51.5 million adults experience mental illness each year.

Although society is making mild efforts toward change, the media often leads us to believe you can look at someone and know they are depressed.

By the time you can see the visible signs of depression, these feelings have been carried for a significant period. Let's be real, at times, we can easily glance past our own signs of depression. For instance, we can spend most of the day appearing to be fine, but if the people around us would listen closely, our conversations are drenched in worry and regret.

We procrastinate and put off seemingly small tasks that now feel overwhelming.

Depression can move us from feeling energized to struggling and negotiating when to get out of bed each morning. Then to balance our physical system we may increase our consumption of caffeine and become determined to increase productivity. We tell ourselves as long as we keep up the expected pace, there is no threat, but *denial is one of the most dangerous vulnerabilities of all.*

Uninstall unnecessary programming.

* * * *

When we perform a system update, it is also an optimal time to increase the system's capacity. In the world of technology this is called increasing the solid-state drive (Solodov and Solodov 2021). It often involves running a virus protection scan that will tell us if there are any hidden programs running or critical files that should be deleted. We will then be given data on the system's memory and how much space is available to use.

A device's speed and efficiency are often directly correlated to the amount of available space on its hard drive. If the hard drive is near capacity, programs run slowly, making everything you do seem more difficult than necessary.

More importantly, if the storage is full, there's no room for the critical updates that will keep the system in balance. Are you catching on to the analogy? We can all benefit from this protocol of removing pointless programming.

Now, wouldn't it be wonderful if our mirrors had a blinking neon sign that said, "UPDATES AVAILABLE?" Yes, I said neon, because some of us are so stubborn that if the message isn't loud and clear we will walk right past it.

The good news is our system is designed to let us know when it is out of balance.

Mentally we will struggle to concentrate, and our thinking patterns become like dominoes of worst-case scenarios. Physically, digestive problems, chronic pain, changes in our heart rate, and low libido can all signal it's time to check for updates.

The physical warnings of a potential system crash are crucial to acknowledge and address.

We can say all the right things and verbally proclaim our "solid-state" is intact, but our body will not disguise the truth. It will fire off in various ways until we slow down and pay attention.

The presence of anxiety and depression are often unwelcome, but the state of our bodies during these conditions are designed to save our lives. These moments propel us to figure out what thoughts and experiences take up too much space, reduce our mental clutter, and make room for hope and possibility. There comes a point where pushing restart won't be enough.

All the ongoing patches and fixes we've made will no longer be compatible with our long-term functioning. This is the moment where we must consider an update, or a shift, and in the process of the transition identify what expired mindsets hide in the background, what mindsets will we carry forward, and which ones hold us back. This is the critical moment where shifting our mindset will mark the beginning of moving from reacting to reimagining.

System updates available.

RESTORE:

Please always remember to take agency as you engage in these mindfulness practices. They are optional and meant to support your work as you engage through this book. Honor your effort and know there is no right or wrong way to work through this exercise. Just notice and be curious about how you move through each passing moment.

FIVE MINUTE MINDFULNESS

If possible, sit up straight with your head balanced on your neck and your shoulders stacked over your hips. This posture aligns our neuromuscular body and opens up your blood flow. Another option would be to lie on your back with your knees bent and the soles of your feet on the floor.

Find a comfortable posture that you can maintain without strain for three to five minutes.

Allow your eyes to close or gaze downward.

Minute 1 – The act of breathing is underrated and taken for granted. Focus on your breath and feel the air fill your body.

Minute 2 – Pay attention to where your breath goes and notice your reaction to being present with yourself. Notice any bodily sensations.

Minute 3 – Now become aware of your thoughts and ask yourself, "How am I really doing?" Then without judgment, try to allow the answers to this question to surface.

Minute 4 – Move your attention toward awareness of your emotions. Can you allow your breathing, your body, and your thoughts/emotions to coexist? (This can be more challenging than it sounds, just stay with it)

Minute 5 – Return your focus to your breathing, concentrating on the inhale and the exhale.

REFLECT:

In your experience, how does it typically work out when you are too determined to do things your own way?

If possible, describe some of your vulnerabilities. These are the social dynamics and situations that make it difficult to maintain your health and well-being.

What do you know about your physical body and the way it reacts when you are stressed and overwhelmed?

Where in your life are you tired of pushing restart? What might be different if you could make a lasting change in this area?

RECALIBRATE:

The Mindset: I should be able to overcome my challenges on my own.

*Use the space below to develop a **mental shift** statement and recalibrate your perspective on the mindset above:*

When Your Wall Becomes a Fortress

——

The Mindset: If this keeps happening to me, it must be my fault.

Shortly after my daughter Cierra turned twenty-one, she and I had a valuable conversation that transcends age and time. It was centered around our internal beliefs and how they can keep us standing in our own way.

At the time, she was a junior in college and felt life was moving like a bullet train. The other side of her college career was just around the corner and with the uncertainty of the future came doubt. As she thought about her life and some of her interactions with others, she felt frustrated and overlooked.

From her perspective, everyone else seemed comfortable and confident and easily engaged with one another, while she sat back quietly and watched. Trapped by the internal tug of war that seemed to control her mind, she often felt partially present, like a shell of herself.

Socially, she could feel her discomfort and desire to withdraw, but also felt powerless to change. She was resigning to the belief, "This is just how I am."

As much as she tried to see that statement as true, it never brought the resolve she desired. The internal anxiety she battled was a primary source of self-criticism and ran parallel to her concerns over the judgment of others.

Whenever she walked into a room, she was already met with assumptions based on the way she looked, the way she spoke, or the general stereotypes people would freely voice. Blind to her battle, a few people in her circle of peers "encouraged" her to consider that being quiet could make her come off as rude or unapproachable.

It broke my heart when I heard what she was told, and I wanted the names and locations of those "friends" I needed to put in their place! Having this conversation by phone was my saving grace and kept my mama bear from coming out! I could hide the anger that lit my face on fire and allow my eyes to tear up while still holding space for her heart.

Why is being quiet perceived as disrespectful?

Who wrote the rules that dictate how we show up and move through the world? Do people realize how exhausting it can be to show up and make everyone comfortable, but yourself?

Particularly in the American ethos, there is culture of personality that misunderstands and diminishes temperaments that don't exude social extroversion (Cain 2012). In other words, when people don't act and perform in ways that validate our level of comfort, we may develop negative stereotypes toward their character and personality.

Cierra went on to say, "I work so hard to do what's uncomfortable and push myself to be what everyone expects. I fight through anxiety and show up with a smile. Will it ever stop being so painful?"

There was a brief moment of silence and then I replied, "Yes. That's a pressure you don't have to carry. When you can walk into a room and take pride in your nature, the fear of rejection won't hold as much power. It sounds like you've convinced yourself that disengaging from your peers will ensure you don't get hurt."

If avoidance were bricks, Cierra had built a strong and mighty wall, and now the wall she built had become a fortress. She had convinced herself she simply enjoyed being alone and had no interest in taking risks to build relationships.

Symbolically, her wall was an attempt to relieve the tension between her desire to belong and her fear of rejection.

Her *wall* was a collection of self-protective behaviors such as minimizing her feelings and over-adapting to the demands of others. These patterns of behaviors became her way of avoiding potentially threatening situations. It was a classic case of cognitive dissonance, where an individual holds contradictory beliefs to separate themselves from truths they don't want to face (Barlow, Durand, and Hoffman, 2018).

Cognitive dissonance isn't always easy to recognize, but it can be a common response to situations that create conflict. When a person's beliefs and behaviors are incongruent, they may resort to the following:

- explaining away conflict.
- hiding beliefs to minimize feelings of shame and guilt.
- avoiding new information that contradicts what they want to believe.
- surrounding themselves with people who will always agree with their opinions.

True to our relationship, Cierra was quick to become defensive. She insisted, "Oh no, it's not rejection!"

So, I rephrased, "Your silence is an attempt not to be seen, but it's also the opposite of what you really want. The fear of not measuring up to the people around you makes you question the value of showing them who you are."

Her silence let me know I hit the nail on the head.

For Cierra, transparency had proven to be dangerous. It lured her into relationships filled with unanticipated manipulation and rejection. Matched with her desire to please, these repeated occurrences led to feelings of inadequacy and self-blame.

Cierra had come to believe, *if this keeps happening to me, it must be my fault.*

* * * *

Holding our emotions inside and drawing conclusions that lead to self-blame can create an unhealthy pattern of internalization. When this pattern is dominant, we take on the faults of others because we are unwilling to see the truth of their character or hold them responsible for change.

Self-blame *is the ultimate form of emotional abuse* and exaggerates our perceived inadequacies to a point of emotional destruction (Real but Not True, 2017).

When it involves those we love or hold in high regard, this cycle of response can be difficult to break. Our minds may struggle to accept that no matter what we do, it's not enough. Even when it's a parent or spouse, there's a chance they don't have the capacity to consistently meet our needs. What they withhold may say more about *their* brokenness than it does about *your* worth.

Engaging in self-blame, as a way of maintaining hope, is a dangerous game to play. It becomes an open door to the *if-then cycle,* where you become overly determined to secure relational connection.

If this cycle involves a toxic relationship, additional blame may be directed your way. You may be told, *"If you didn't act that way, then I wouldn't get upset"* or *"If you weren't so sensitive this wouldn't be a problem."*

Anyone can fall prey to the blame game, but it is commonly observed in those who are empathetic, highly sensitive, or demonstrate a high need to please (Patil et al., 2017). A consistent loop of self-blame may also indicate strong feelings of unworthiness and fear of failure.

Consider your history of assuming self-blame and explore your answers to these questions:

- When did this mindset begin to take root in my life?
- Has the constant assumption of self-blame proven to be beneficial?
- How am I taking responsibility for circumstances I didn't create?
- In what ways am I critical and demeaning toward myself?
- What evidence do I have that I'm solely responsible for the dynamics in this relationship?

＊ ＊ ＊ ＊

Have you ever felt connected to someone and later realized you were the glue that held it all together? They loved everything you brought to the table, and as long as you didn't ask for much in return, they were all in. You were a constant in their lives, but they would become disinterested or unavailable when you reached out for support.

These types of relationships can fly under the radar because they offer just enough crumbs to keep you hungry for more. The blend of opposing personalities may also create a complementary, though unhealthy bond.

One person is the "giver" who finds value in being needed and the other is a "taker" who feels entitled to have their needs met. By the time the "giver" is willing to acknowledge their mistreatment, they have been emotionally manipulated. They are no longer confident they can trust their instinct.

Your identity and temperament are worthy of appreciation and respect. They will naturally flourish when you're in a healthy environment. Reject the lie that says you ask for too much or that it's your fault because you're not enough. When someone wants to be a part of your life, you won't have to beg them to stay. Find people who choose you the way you choose them because trust is built on the other side of the *wall*. It will develop when you can move beyond your protective wall and feel safe to be yourself.

Walking away from defense patterns can feel like a big risk, but this shift isn't meant to place you in the line of fire. Moving through life with relational flexibility can be a helpful way to update your perspective.

Relational flexibility allows you to stay in a place of neutrality as you interact and connect with the people in your life. As you grow and evolve, you will assess and determine the type of personal and professional relationships that support your current season. You will become an observer of others' actions and adjust the level of access they have to your life. There will be a progressive detachment from taking things personally and believing the way you're treated is contingent upon your worth.

Use these questions to guide your exploration into relational flexibility:

- What do I need in my interpersonal relationships to feel they are secure? (personally and professionally)
- How do the people in my life support me through difficult times?
- In what ways have I adapted or changed to maintain certain relationships?
- How have these changes influenced other areas of my life? What do I think about myself?
- Are there any parts of myself I diminish or hide to feel congruent with my peers? If so, why?
- Who are the people in my life that support *both* my present and my future?

In your mind imagine a bullseye with your name written in the center. Surrounding it are the names of the most important people in your life. Then strategically consider where you'd place the other people in your world and why.

Think about the common characteristics among those in your inner circle. Is there anyone who needs to be positioned farther out? If you had to follow through with this change, could you? We hold responsibility for positioning people in our lives, and we must take honest inventory of how we allow ourselves to be treated.

Not everyone deserves full privilege and access to your life.

Be mindful that new connections are designed to begin on the outer ring of our relational bullseye. The space provides us a chance to observe our patterns of attachment and make better decisions around who we let in our lives.

If we lose sight of who we are or diminish what it means to walk in our shoes, we run the risk of attracting people who hold space but aren't compatible with our lives.

Consider taking time to step back and define what you need to feel authentic and connected. Notice any thoughts that rise to the surface, especially those that are filled with doubt. Consider contexts such as your season of life, temperament, values, and expectations. Relationships can either perpetuate our struggles or help create the conditions we need to heal. They are an integral part of mental health, at every age.

* * * *

Cierra tore down the walls of her fortress and moved beyond the dim and depressed light. She no longer woke up suffocated by anxiety and fighting to make it through the day.

On the other side of the wall, the sun was bright, and the grass was green; life felt brighter than before. Her point of reference had changed, and her vision was now clear.

As she continued to ground in her new reality, she braced for the feelings of regret and shame. The past reflected choices she thought she'd never make, and the memories held hurt she never expected to bear.

As a mother I reminded her, "*Healing takes patience* and we're allowed to show ourselves compassion through any part of the storm."

No magic switch turns off the scenes along our road of regret. Staying mindfully in the present means detaching from our suffering and resisting intimacy with our pain. Keeping our mind focused on our faults may convince us we don't deserve to experience joy.

It's not about what you deserve, but rather your willingness to draw the line and move out of your own way. Playing small doesn't keep you safe; it keeps you comfortable and complacent. It will talk you out of your destiny and keep you trapped in comparison.

Hope is waiting to remind you there are better things ahead than what you've left behind. Stop waiting for permission to stand rooted in your worth and declare,

I release myself from the version of me I created to survive.

RESTORE:

Please always remember to take agency as you engage in these mindfulness practices. They are optional and meant to support your work as you engage through this book. Honor what your mind and body need, while working to show gratitude for the courage it takes to show up for yourself. It is best to read through this exercise and then begin.

GENTLE GROUNDING TECHNIQUE
Notice your breathing. Try not to control it, but just notice the pace and depth of your breathing. Can you give yourself permission to spend time in the moment without judgment?

As you stay connected to your breathing *inhale through your nose* and notice the way the air feels as it enters your body.

Pause.

Exhale through your mouth and notice the way your body feels as the air releases.

Continue breathing, now working to lengthen each breath.

INHALE and think about what you want to experience more. Imagine yourself bringing it into your life. What would be different about the way you think? Act? Speak to yourself?

EXHALE and imagine yourself releasing what you no longer want to carry. This may be thoughts, habits, or even relationships.

Use this exercise to practice visualization and harnessing your ability of choice. You must first believe you can choose what comes in and out of your life before you will be willing to take steps toward bringing it to life.

REFLECT:

What assumptions do YOU make about how you're viewed by others?

How would you describe your current community of friendships and how much of your full self do they get to experience?

What are your *automatic default settings*, your immediate thoughts, and responses when you feel rejected or like an outsider?

Who are the people in your life that offer support and encouragement when you make changes? Who are the people that tend to make you second guess yourself during seasons of change?

RECALIBRATE:

The Mindset: If this keeps happening to me, it must be my fault.

Use the space below to develop a ***mental shift*** to help recalibrate your perspective on the mindset above:

Making Peace with Your Shadow

———

The Mindset: If I focus on being positive, everything else will take care of itself.

In late 2019, my daughter, Cierra, was nineteen years old. Just a few months away from her December birthday, she began to make some exciting plans.

Although she was our oldest, we were doing pretty well in the cutting-the-cord department. She and her friends planned a short beach getaway, and we adjusted to the reality of her celebrating without us.

Nearly a year later, in September 2020, Cierra found the courage to write the narrative below and emotionally revisit what she considered the calm before the storm. The challenges she faced in 2020 had shifted her perspective and *made it difficult to remember what joy and connection were like.*

Looking back was now a reminder of what had been lost.

Cierra's recollection of her birthday weekend is below.

The December evening air felt crisp against my skin as I trudged slowly through the sand of Wrightsville Beach. Following close behind was a camaraderie of both old and new friends, as well as a few random strangers I'd met over the weekend. Our new-found companionship, much like the washed up seashells that lined the shore, was simply a result of luck—or maybe even fate. Though my feet sunk through the sand with every step, I couldn't help but feel light on my toes as I danced with the waves to the rhythm of the Earth. My curls seemed to fly both left to right, sticking to my lip gloss as a breeze swept through the air. I wrapped myself tighter in my Aztec throw blanket and let out a shiver as we moved closer to the water. The sky was painted in hues of purples, pinks, and oranges that seemed to kiss the edges of the sea. Lost in the beauty of the moment, I fell deeply in love with a mirage of perfection, of which I now know to be a useless desire.

It was New Year's Eve and the night before I had just turned twenty. I had always loved having a birthday that fell just two days before the beginning of a new year. It fulfilled my wish to live life as though it were a storybook, with my birthday marking the start of each new chapter. We planned to stop by the beach to watch the sunset before the nighttime festivities began. With nothing but a Bluetooth speaker and a few blankets, the seven of us sought out a small adventure.

We didn't know that our rather last-minute decision to kill time throughout our eventless evening would be one of the very last times we would experience face-to-face human interaction. Had we known, maybe we would have stayed longer and held each other a little tighter. Standing just a few feet away from the shoreline, I watched as the waves seemed to move closer and closer to where I stood. The wet sand beneath my feet acted as a bridge between me and the ocean's ebb and flow while the song "Fine Line" by Harry Styles played softly in the background. Without realizing, we had all gone silent. The sound of crashing waves and soft music blending together in perfect harmony. I looked to my left to see some of my friends holding each other, swaying slowly to the beat. I'm not much of a hugger, but I wish I would've hugged someone that day.

The next six minutes and eighteen seconds felt endless—until it wasn't. Later that night, I'd put on a sparkly two piece set, with pink eyeshadow and my hair pulled back in a tight low ponytail. My friends and I would get all the way to the club just to realize that I'd left my ID at the apartment. I spent the final moments of 2019 frantically searching for my wallet and making it back to the club with just three minutes left until the ball dropped. I'd squeeze through the crowd of small beach town locals to finally be reunited with my friends.

"Ten, nine, eight..."

I didn't know that the seemingly perfect night was but a prelude to the hardships to come the following year.

"Seven, six, five, four..."

I'd unknowingly celebrate the forthcoming of my highest highs and lowest lows.

"Three, two, one… Happy New Year!"

I didn't know that 2020 would be a year far from the imagined futures and fantasies seen through rose colored glasses that only blurred my judgment. <u>I didn't know that I would spend months visiting the darkest parts of my own mind, yearning for the peace that day brought me</u>. I didn't know that I would go on long drives to listen to "Fine Line" on repeat. That I would sit and remind myself that life is but a fleeting moment—an ebb and flow that naturally wanes through seasons of sadness and joy, solitude and company, pain and pleasure leaving me with no other option than to dance on the fine line in between.

* * * *

These were her last moments of peace before Cierra came face to face with her shadow—the hidden parts of her being. She, like many of us, had no idea what 2020 would bring. More importantly, she was unprepared and overwhelmed by the complexities of what she discovered about herself that year.

The idea of the shadow self was created by psychologist Carl Jung. According to Jung, our shadow is the part of ourselves we try to repress and hide, fearing that if seen, our weaknesses will be on full display. It is the psychological term for everything we can't see in ourselves. The shadow symbolizes the parts of ourselves we struggle to accept or those parts we've been conditioned to label socially unacceptable (Masters 2018).

Cierra has always been introspective and mildly aware of her hidden nature, but she expressed 2020 thrust her into a tug of war.

Her present reality was filled with loss, social isolation, racial and political conflict, and confusion. Then in unfortunate parallel, *seeking clarity illuminated elements of her past that were clearly not healed.* **Her best attempts at remaining positive were no longer enough,** but the thought of fully giving in to her shadow was terrifying.

Like Cierra, you may wonder, *if you choose to uncover what hides in the dark, how will you be judged by those who see you in the light?*

An unexpected benefit to Cierra's shadow work was gaining this awareness early in life. According to 2019 research conducted by the National Alliance on Mental Illness (NAMI), half of all lifetime mental health conditions begin by age fourteen and 75 percent by age twenty-four. However, fewer than half of all adults seek out any level of support to manage their mental health (NAMI 2020).

Unlike Cierra, my client Sandra was much older and embedded into a lifestyle of toxic positivity that wasn't working out as planned.

* * * *

Sandra was in her late forties and could not figure out why her life felt superficial and stagnant. She told me in our first session, "I feel like I am on the outside looking at a version of myself I don't recognize. I appreciate my life but always have a sense I didn't reach my full potential."

By all accounts she was happily married, enjoying a good life, and she was financially secure.

During our work she frequently mentioned being naturally expressive as a child but recalls constantly being told to calm down or that she was "being too much." As a matter of fact, she was directly told if she didn't learn how to be more mild, other people would not want her around.

This dynamic created a deep well of insecurity and fear Sandra became determined to hide. She was terrified of being alone and determined to be as perfect as possible to gain the approval of others.

Over the years, she became great at meeting the needs of others, but always felt unseen and exhausted by the life she had built. Sandra came to realize she had lost her voice, and now when it was most needed, she was terrified of the repercussions.

Her life was now built around pleasing others by using a watered-down version of her temperament, and she was not sure which was worse—losing what she had built or walking around feeling empty.

Her youngest child was going to leave soon and the lack of connection with her spouse felt like impending doom. Sandra acknowledged she married him because he was safe and always positive, but this also meant they avoided the conversations they needed to have and anything that didn't fit the fantasy was swept under the carpet.

Sandra's mindset is quite common in its aim to only focus on the positive. Whether among casual interactions or in my professional work, "How can I become more positive?" is one of the top requests. I have come across hundreds of people searching for the magic formula to creating the perfect day.

A narrow focus on the positive limits our potential and may set us up for disappointment. A great day means everything has gone as expected and anything outside of this scenario is failure.

An inordinate amount of time is spent crafting the perfect daily routine and timing it down to the minute. No matter what happens, the expectation is to handle it with perfect positivity. To further insulate these beliefs, some will expend countless hours and energy seeking relationships that match this view of positivity.

* * * *

Some of us can relate to not living our truth and presenting a message very different from how we feel inside. We quiet our internal voice and work tirelessly to acquire the achievements, living status, and social circle that will maintain our façade.

Everyone has a different recipe, but the bottom line is most of us are masters of avoidance. We will do everything we can to achieve our perceived standard of greatness while remaining in our comfort zone. Somehow, we have been convinced if we focus on the positive, everything else will take care of itself.

I, like many other historical thought leaders, believe something different.

Carl Jung believed balance can only be achieved when we acknowledge our shadow and learn to authentically integrate our hidden parts into how we show up in the world (Masters 2018). No amount of wealth or accomplishment is a sustainable replacement. When you make peace with your shadow it allows you to harness and access a greater depth of power and potential.

Even love has its limitations. If we are not in a place of love and acceptance, we will doubt the love others attempt to give. Being at war with your shadow is like fighting against your potential. It can block the pathway to personal growth and leave you focused on the wrong perspectives. Is it not exhausting to fight against your potential and to constantly spar with feelings of vulnerability, fear, and shame?

Many of us have an innate desire to believe our life has value, to know we are fulfilling our purpose, and to live out our passions. Moving toward these realities is always within reach, but the road requires us to move from looking to seeing.

When we see ourselves through an open and honest lens it demands a stronger commitment to understanding. Seeing how we acquire meaning sets the stage for our emotional responses. Our shadow is therefore an essential part of seeing beyond the self-image we have created.

I recognize this may sound distressing, and I empathize with my clients who are afraid to do this work. Yet, many of them realize they have been running from their shadow most of their lives and it simply isn't going away. Our shadow has purpose, and much like our subconscious it is present, whether we acknowledge it or not.

* * * *

Recognizing what we believe about our shadow is a helpful place to begin. In my work with clients, some common themes have emerged:

MY SHADOW SHOULD BE FEARED.

Every emotion has value and fear can shift us into resolve and action. We fear our shadow because it is our nature to fear uncertainty. However, uncertainty also pushes us to determine what we know and figure out how to gain the answers we seek. The absence of a healthy amount of fear creates a sea of complacency. Over time that complacency comes crashing in as waves of regret.

Consider Tim, who experienced a bad break up during his first year of college. He was not only devastated but determined he would never allow this to happen again. Fearful of allowing any emotional vulnerability, he put up invisible barriers that kept him from fully connecting with others. This same mindset seeped into his professional life, and he became unwilling to make any vocational changes that involved risk or required him to build connections with colleagues.

Now approaching fifty-five, Tim had spent his entire adult life alone and had very few friends. Over the past ten years he battled depression, which was often masked as anger and aggression. He was also consumed with guilt and ashamed to be at a point where he needed help. Tim was also filled with regret, constantly looking back and verbally beating himself up for the missed opportunities he now desperately desired. Both Tim and his shadow were in desperate need of compassion.

MY SHADOW IS A REFLECTION OF WHO I AM.

A shadow is not a reflection even though it is the same shape as the object. One of biggest reasons we avoid facing our shadow is because we don't want to believe what it reveals. Your shadow is <u>not who you are</u> exposing everything about your shortcomings. That is the deception!

Your shadow is the hidden manifestation of your pain, your trauma, or any neglect you have experienced. It is a projection that illuminates whether we are in everyday interactions or experiencing high levels of psychological and/or physiological stress.

After Nicole lost her brother in a car accident, she felt as though part of herself had died as well. She withdrew from friends and family and threw herself into her work. Nicole used her job, and eventually food, as a means of staying emotionally numb. In her mind, the exhaustion of work and the physical pain of binge eating was better than dealing with the reality of life without her brother.

This avoidance was unsustainable and a few years after her brother's death, Nicole hit a wall. She barely recognized the person in the mirror and couldn't remember the last time she slept through the night. I was able to help Nicole understand who she had become within the context of her pain. Together, we were able to identify the daily actions that added to her struggles. Nicole needed to be reminded of who she was before her brother died and give herself permission to live.

THE PRESENCE OF MY SHADOW IS A SIGN OF WEAKNESS/FAILURE.

The closer an object is to the light the larger the shadow appears. Symbolically, the light represents hope. It represents the presence of the things in our life that are bigger than our fears—the motivations that keep us pushing. When your shadow feels like a giant, it's not always a sign you're heading in the wrong direction. Yes, light magnifies our darkness, but it also makes us choose whether we will yield to our fears or believe that something better is possible.

When Kelli and I first met, she expressed being more vulnerable and willing to look at herself than ever before. Her actions supported her words, but she didn't expect it to be so difficult. In particular, she was working on setting boundaries with people who manipulated her kindness. It was devastating for Kelli to realize some of her closest friends were the primary offenders in her life. If her process of growth were coming at such a high cost, Kelli questioned if it would be worth the price.

* * *

Staying in a place of resistance and attempting to ignore our inner pain is like aligning with self-sabotage. In some instances, we can even dramatize our pain and use it as an excuse to maintain our patterns.

A common example of this resistance pattern is when we seek intimacy and connection with those who are emotionally unavailable. If we subconsciously believe we aren't worthy of love and once found, it will not stay, then settling for shallow encounters becomes a damaging act of self-protection.

In his book, *Bringing Your Shadow Out of the Dark,* Dr. Robert Augustus Masters (2018) reminds us, "Our shadow doesn't contain just our unpleasant or far-from flattering qualities, but often some of our finest qualities and capacities." When we make peace with our shadow it allows us to challenge the resistance that has kept us from experiencing freedom. It increases our ability to meet our resistance with compassion, reducing the heaviness and burden we feel forced to carry.

Walking in peace with our shadow makes us more willing to take risks. These risks help test our limits, push beyond our limitations, and abandon the belief we are destined for failure. When we step out of our comfort zone, it clarifies our desires, making us more likely to achieve our goals.

Whether you've told yourself the cards are stacked against you, or you have felt bullied by your shadow self, I believe hope can be found buried beneath your fears. If you're the "strong one," take off your own cape. The downside to being the "strong one" is you're not always given the same space to fall apart.

Create the space you need—the space you so freely create for others. Be the hero or heroine of your own story without the condition of saving everyone else first. If you have seen parts of your shadow that scare you, or you fear the darkness you hide may prove stronger than the light, what if your conclusions are wrong? What if your fear is a mirage or a smoke screen? Perhaps what you actually fear is your greatness and the responsibility of living up to your potential on a consistent basis.

At a certain point we have to stop making excuses and waiting for the right moment. We must choose to listen and act on the changes that try to pull us forward. Resisting the reality of change maintains a state of denial, which is a defense mechanism in the face of fear. Give in to the providence of this moment and bring your shadow out of the dark. Be relentless in your pursuit of peace and do whatever it takes to heal the distorted views and destructive patterns that weigh you down. On the other side of fear is the freedom you need to move you forward.

Let fear become your fuel.

RESTORE:

Today we will add visualization to our meditative breath work. Visualization is one of the most powerful and overlooked methods of changing our narrative and automatic beliefs. It changes how our brain organizes information and improves connection between different areas of the brain.

I encourage you to read through this exercise before you begin and to repeat it as often as you desire. Take whatever posture or position feels good to your body, as long as you are relaxed. Remember, this is optional and here to enhance your experience. If this mindfulness practice becomes uncomfortable at any time, honor your need to stop.

- Breathe deeply.
- Allow yourself to become aware of your thoughts toward your shadow—the parts of yourself you don't want to be seen.
- Allow these thoughts without judgment or changing them.
- Now take one issue you seek to hide and visualize yourself in a situation where this issue is met with care. Imagine you are in a situation where this issue is now a strength.
- Stay in this visualization as long as you can, working to add details to the picture in your mind.
- Stay connected to your breathing.
- When you are ready, slowly bring yourself back into the present moment and bring your awareness back into your space.
- Notice how your body feels after intentional breath work and visualization. (Repeat exercise as desired)

REFLECT:

1. What are your beliefs about the power of positivity?

2. How has your ability to be positive been helpful? How has it created any challenges?

3. Which parts of yourself do you work to keep hidden? Why?

4. How would your life be different if you fully accepted the parts of yourself you consider flaws?

RECALIBRATE:

The Mindset: If I focus on being positive, everything else will take care of itself.

*Use the space below to develop a **mental shift** statement that will help recalibrate the mindset above:*

CH.10

The Difference Is You

——

The Mindset: There's nothing special about my life. Does my voice really matter?

When we moved to Charlotte, North Carolina, in April 2006 our neighbor, Tempe, was one of the first people to extend her friendship. She also had a son close to my daughter's age and they had a sweet bond during the first few years of the transition.

It was a normal day in 2019 when Tempe reached out through social media and encouraged me to apply for the first annual Anne Boyd Moore Scholarship to the Excellence in Speaking Institute (ESI). This scholarship was sponsored by Ty Boyd, Inc., an executive communication and coaching business that has supported professionals worldwide for forty years.

I looked up the site and my immediate reaction was doubt and skepticism. This looked way out of my league and competing for the scholarship would push me well outside of my comfort zone. I, unlike many of the other applicants, didn't have the built-in support of being a member of a larger business or organization. I'm also one of the least competitive people in the world. While I would undoubtedly benefit from the training, there was a part of me that felt on the surface, everything about it was wrong. It didn't seem like a good fit.

That same evening as I lay down for the night, I began to question if there was more than coincidence to this moment. My mother always taught me to trust in God's ability to orchestrate my life and to place experiences before me that were meant for my good. I was coming off a year of big changes and could sense I was a little out of steam. Within the past year, I transitioned from a job, opened my own business, and began working on my PhD.

The next morning, I took some time to google Anne Boyd Moore, the name of the woman who the scholarship honored. Anne was the eldest daughter of Ty Boyd and served as CEO of the international communication and coaching business up until her battle with cancer made it difficult. Anne lost her battle with cancer in 2017 and reading about her life demonstrated the legacy of love she had left behind.

Her family wrote about her journey and emphasized, "Anne faced her uphill battle in the same manner as she lived her life—with strength, courage, grace, and love." After I read this line, I thought to myself, Anne's fight sounds reminiscent of someone I know—my mother. I couldn't walk away from this door without trying.

I want you to recognize how important it is to stay open to the unexpected. There will be integral moments in your journey where seemingly small and unintentional occurrences will shift the entire trajectory of your life. They will not always be packaged in familiar form, and the odds may seem stacked against you, but stay open to possibility.

Reach forward, even if you're afraid.

* * * *

I knew my biggest hurdle would be soliciting votes from friends and colleagues, since the winner would be based on the number of online votes received. I struggle with self-promotion, so I had to figure out how to shift my perspective around what made me apprehensive. How could I translate this into an effort that felt more authentic to who I was?

Through a combination of the support of those who believed in my vision and sharing parts of my own story, I completed ten days of campaigning for votes.

This came through posting social media posts on various platforms, sending daily email video messages to share my passion for speaking, and even asking a few friends and those I have supported, to create videos of support on my behalf. It was terrifying and exhausting!

There were moments I wanted to back down, but the vision I had for the future pulled me through. This process also took a significant amount of self-talk, and I had to challenge the voice of doubt that attempted to take center stage.

When we find ourselves focused on counterproductive thoughts, we can use temporal distancing, which is the process of thinking about how you will feel when the situation is over (Liberman, Sagristano, and Trope, 2007). To engage in this process, you can also go back to a time where you had a similar feeling and overcame the situation. This is a valuable way to decrease the pressure of the moment.

To prevent myself from getting caught up in a tornado of doubt, I engaged in temporal distancing. I took time to think about past experiences that were overwhelming and outside of my comfort zone but ended successfully. When using this intervention with clients, these questions help guide their process:

- Briefly describe or bring the past experience to mind.
- How did you assume it would turn out?
- What specific mindsets or coping skills helped you experience success?
- How can you translate lessons from that experience to the situation you're working through now?

A few days after the voting window closed, I was shocked and overwhelmed when I received the email announcing I won. There was a surge of apprehension shooting through my body, but I was also filled with excitement. No one knew the significance of this opportunity. I had a big passion project I felt called to bring to life. For the past six months I had quietly been praying for the resources needed to make it happen. I had a natural gift for speaking, well established from years of talking in class, but I was at the point where life called for more.

Our natural gifts will only take us so far without intentional development. To enhance my ability and understanding of higher-level communication, I needed help. There was a new season approaching and I didn't want to miss it because I was determined to figure it out on my own.

* * * *

From the moment I walked into the first day of ESI, it was an experience. Molly Hunt and Dave Reinhardt, PhD, were the two facilitators. Let me tell you, they were everything I didn't know I needed in my life!

When Molly spoke, I found myself hanging on her every word, caught up in the imagery she created and the emotions of the stories she shared. When she spoke, it was more genuine than I expected, and she clearly demonstrated excellence in her craft.

Dave was tall and slender with a smile that immediately brightened the room. He used humor to help create a unique learning experience and for me, this was a powerful reminder that dimming your light is not an indicator of excellence.

In my one-on-one time with Dave, his brilliance was striking and gave me an extensive amount of clarity. I was a passionate speaker, but this emotion was somewhat scattered, and I would touch on too many different topics within a given timeframe. Dave helped me learn the balance of maintaining my personality, while staying focused on one central message.

There were also parts of my story I desperately wanted to share, but my personal and professional "rules" often felt like opposing forces. As therapists we are often encouraged to limit personal disclosure, yet I have always felt my story holds significance for the unconditional regard I extend to clients. I recognize the need to moderate disclosure during therapy, but I felt there was another lane I needed to create where personal and professional could appropriately intersect.

Molly and Dave's guidance handed me the keys to the internal doors I had been struggling to unlock. They helped empower me with the technical skills and techniques to walk confidently into new territory. This is what great coaches do. They enhance your ability and help you optimize your impact.

Every moment of training was meticulous, intentional, and filled with a beautiful balance of push and pull. Each member of the cohort was pushed out of their comfort zone and into spontaneous, interactive communication practice. This was always followed by constructive critique that had a gentle way of pulling you through the moment without giving weight to your fears. Among the cohort, there was a universal desire to see each other win and a level of vulnerability and acceptance found more quickly than I had ever experienced.

As you walk into the unknown, remember the value of checking your assumptions at the door. The people around you will play their part, but you make the difference. Your experiences will match your perspective and your perspective will be founded on the mindsets you choose to cultivate.

During the training I could have let my assumptions keep my mind and my body in a place of defense. However, doing so would have greatly diminished my experience. Emotions, like fear and doubt, are also felt within our body, creating physical changes such as sweating, dry mouth, or lightheadedness.

Depending on our comfort level, using our voice or stepping into life transitions can feel like a recipe for a panic attack. To help shield ourselves we can move forward from a place of bias. When we operate from a place of protective bias, we will look to identify every wrong and we will find it at every turn. This mindset shuts down our willingness to be vulnerable and even when physically present, we are emotionally disconnected. Our thoughts are flooded by our inner critic, and we use these messages to rationalize our behavior.

A more adaptive means of personal support is to reassure both our mind and our body we are not truly in a threatening situation. *We can practice mindful awareness of our true thoughts and notice any narratives based in fear.* Then we can intentionally shift our internal dialogue by refocusing our thoughts toward hope and becoming open to the possibility we can succeed. As this occurs, our body will often follow and move toward a greater place of calm.

In *My Grandmother's Hands,* author Resmaa Menakem highlights the ways in which the soul nerve, also known as the vagus nerve, is a central part of the intersection between human behavior and the nervous system. The soul nerve is where we experience the physical, felt sense of our emotional experiences whether it is a sense of compassion and joy, or despair and disgust. This is important to understand because your thoughts will influence your behaviors, and together they will send messages to your soul nerve, cueing self-protective behaviors or spreading the message you are safe and can relax (Menakem, 2017).

These messages impact your health and well-being, regulate your breathing and heart rate, and even influence your mood (Van Der Kolk 2014). Our environment plays a role in our ability to exchange and operate from healthier mindsets, but we are the greatest agent of change. Igniting this shift is up to us, and our body is one of the most honest indicators of how we experience this awakening.

Our story, even the parts that create feelings of shame, disappointment, or regret, is still ultimately designed to be one of our greatest sources of power. If we are unable to accept the fullness of our lives, we will constantly doubt the ability for others to do the same.

Sadly, this resistance will also symbolically enter the room before us, attempting to capitalize on the negative messages from our inner critic.

Your work is to stare those messages in the face and challenge them. When you give yourself permission to view your hidden stories through a wider lens, you will begin to understand your responses, especially those you repeat despite the pain they cause.

Communication is the one of the most powerful tools we have, but all power must be harnessed. How we communicate with ourselves will directly influence our confidence or lack thereof in communicating with others. Deficiencies in this area can hurt us both personally and professionally. This is an invitation to abandon the habit of silencing your story and quieting your voice.

Your story holds a unique perspective only you can give. Having or desiring a speaking platform is not required to validate our story's worth.

My ESI experience was not about professional leverage. It was about harnessing my power so it could be used to encourage the people I love and support. Life has a way of trying to convince us being quiet ensures our safety, but silence is betrayal because our voice has the power to save lives.

* * * *

Through our silence, our actions, or a combination of both, we are still seen. The concept of hiding and attempting to be invisible is not plausible. Our story is shared and communicated through the subtle experiences and interactions within our daily encounters. It is shared through how we lead and how we love or the ways in which we attempt to hide.

At every moment, some version of your story is on display, but you make the difference in the version of yourself communicated to the world. Allow yourself to aim higher.

Civil rights leader Benjamin E. Mays says it well: "The tragedy of life is not found in failure but complacency. Not in you doing too much but doing too little. Not in you living above your means, but below your capacity. It's not about failure but aiming too low, that is life's greatest tragedy" (Thurman, 2021).

ESI participants would often have an opportunity to meet the founder, Ty Boyd. However, at the time of my training this was no longer the practice. About six weeks after my ESI experience, Ty Boyd passed away, which made me even more honored to be a tiny part of his living legacy. I was a direct recipient of his life and willingness to make a difference in others. His written and spoken words are filled with enthusiasm and intention, as he harnesses the power found in every story he shares.

Through his legacy and my experiences with Molly and Dave, I felt as if I was given the missing pieces to a puzzle. Taking the risk to compete, pushing past my fears, and remaining open to the unknown were choices I had to make to create the conditions for growth. Those same choices are before you every day.

In *The Million Dollar Toolbox,* written by Ty Boyd, he discusses the power of effective communication and how it can be used to tap into the energy and passion we have that can change our world. He speaks of learning to manage your fears instead of allowing them to manage you, because once they are in check, anything is possible. The book also includes powerful perspectives on "the impossible goal of perfection" and eliminating the desire for perfection or even the desire to play it safe (Boyd, 2002).

Instead, one of our most powerful tools is to work, to build on our mistakes, and recognize it as progress. Perfection is unattainable and playing it safe will keep us parked in neutral. How many times have you already found yourself bouncing back and forth between perfection and safety? We all choose our direction and have a unique role to play and honor in life. Yet, it requires diligence and determination because in the wise words of Ty Boyd, "If we don't own our lane, someone else will."

Harness your power.

RESTORE:

EXTEND YOUR GAZE

I encourage you to read through this exercise before you begin and to repeat it as often as you desire. Take whatever posture or position feels good to your body, as long as you are relaxed. Remember, this is optional and here to enhance your experience. If this mindfulness practice becomes uncomfortable at any time, honor your need to stop.

If possible, find an area where you can sit comfortably in a dimly lit or dark space. Place a small lit candle in the center of the room or on a secure surface a few feet away from your gaze. Adjust the placement of the candle and notice how your body responds to where it is placed. Settle in on the location where you sit back and feel grounded when the candle is within your sight.

- Now let's begin.

- Draw your eyes toward the candle and keep them open, with a gentle gaze. You may close them if that's more comfortable.
- Connect with your breathing and bring your attention to how the air is moving through your body. Imagine that it can move freely and expansively.
- Inhale and exhale at a rhythm and pace that feels good in your body.
- Complete the statement, I am _____. Choose words that speak to the shifts you desire in your thoughts. You may say this phrase in your mind or aloud.
- Continue breathing and every so often, repeat your statement of power.

REFLECT:

What are your thoughts toward accepting help? What conditions do you place on the people you allow to support you?

How do you typically handle new experiences, especially those that involve personal risk and vulnerability?

What do you truly believe about the value of your life story?

How much confidence do you have in your ability to make the greatest difference in your life? What makes you feel this way?

If you had a greater sense of confidence, what would you do differently?

RECALIBRATE:

The Mindset: There's nothing special about my life. Does my voice really matter?

*Use the space below to develop a **mental shift** to help recalibrate your perspective on the mindset above:*

Reclaim Your Breath

The Mindset: No matter what I do,
people constantly let me down.

At the beginning of our journey through these pages, there was an invitation to broaden and deepen your **awareness** of the hidden mindsets in your life. Many of our beliefs are held within the conscious mind, but disregarded and unresolved experiences will always call for our attention. The unique intricacy of our human design allows us to reconcile our past and our present, so we can improve our future.

This can influence the way we show up in the world and activate a greater source of potential. May we never lose sight of this reality and the ability we have to transform how we experience life. We are not bound to repeating the patterns that weigh us down and act as roadblocks. Every day is a chance to take **action** by making peace with our shadow and shifting our thoughts and responses to help reorganize our neural pathways.

Every part of our day holds purpose and will move us either toward or away from reaching our potential. So how do we stay focused and engaged in this transformative work? First, we need to acknowledge our courage and willingness to lean in and be honest about our struggles. It is never easy to unveil the experiences we have buried in the areas of our lives we sometimes feel we can't escape. Making deep internal shifts will require us to dig deep, sustain our pace, and stay committed to our growth when we become weary.

If you already feel this way, don't give up. Your strength can be replenished, especially if you are willing to serve yourself a notice of **eviction.** We must take a hard look at our rules of engagement and say time's up to the patterns that can no longer be an option. The intensity of our bad experiences does not always lead to giving up our destructive mindsets.

Exhausted by finding ourselves amid the same battles, we often retreat to the exact behaviors that keep us fighting on the front lines. I often see this play out in relationships where we choose different versions of people with similar issues and then can't figure out why we keep getting hurt. It's counterproductive to keep pointing the finger without asking yourself what part you have played in this dynamic.

* * * *

In the book *Song of Solomon*, Toni Morrison writes, "If you want to fly, you have to give up the things that weigh you down." *Letting go* can seem like a simple concept, but many of us have adopted an *if-then mentality.* We want to hold on to our dysfunction and *if* life falls into place, *then* we will release our defense patterns. This mentality has a prerequisite of assurance without risk, which includes making excuses, expecting to fail, and talking ourselves out of our dreams.

Our defense patterns, even if negative, give us a sense of safety. The fear is how can safety be ensured if we abandon these behaviors too soon. So, the goal is reward without risk. We want certainty we won't be hurt, rejected, lose control, or fail, and then we will move forward and not engage in unhealthy coping patterns.

The "if-then" mentality is a roller coaster that cannot produce the consistency you need to make sustainable change. More importantly, this is the classic victim mentality where you accept feeling powerless, live life small, and stay paralyzed by your own limitations.

Oh, how I wish you could hear the current tone in my voice; it's coming from a place of passion and high regard. I'm like the coach who sees you standing just outside of your potential, and I am pumped! Even if you've never considered yourself to be powerful, it is an innate strength you absolutely possess. Sometimes our power is hiding in plain sight, but we've overlooked it because our focus has been in the wrong place. I am determined to help you look beyond your shadow, to dig deep, and bring your power back into view.

You are not your mistakes, your parents' mistakes, or the sum of your regrets. What you believe about yourself will have the greatest impact. Aren't you tired of selling yourself short through playing small? There is an element of fight required for this work, but you are stronger than you think. If you give yourself even a fraction of what you give to others, you will not lose your breath.

* * * *

Grief still meets me at unexpected times. There are moments where I would give anything to pick up the phone and hear my mother's voice because it always made me feel everything would be okay. When I am in the midst of big decisions I crave the confidence my stepfather, Lovell, used to give. In essence, there are times when grief hurts both emotionally and physically. It creates a heaviness and an exhaustion you silently endure because finding the words to explain it never seem adequate.

On November 20, 2020, grief came to visit, and it was brutal. It was the first year of empty nest and the first time I was completely alone on my mother's birthday. My oldest was already back at school and after months of COVID-19-related delays, my youngest had finally been given the green light to head to college. That morning a tight chest and shallow breathing met me like a sunbeam piercing through the clouds. My body felt like a blanket of heaviness, and it was difficult to breathe.

Beneath the surface I felt like I was suffocating. It was as if I could literally feel the ache of pain pumping in my heart along with feeling hollow and numb. I wanted everything to stop and give me time to catch my breath, but time does not play according to our rules. That morning before grief set in, I was already exhausted.

I knew I needed to pace myself instead of pushing through. Pacing myself meant renegotiating my expectations of what it would mean to be productive or even feel strong. On that day, being strong was allowing myself to feel weak. Reviewing my schedule allowed me to determine where I might be asked to provide more than I had to give.

Feelings of guilt were pushed aside, and I resolved to honor my needs without explanation. I didn't have to explain my story as a means of justifying my needs. No one deserved that right, and I wasn't giving anyone that power.

Sometimes, well-meaning people can try to convince us to manage our emotions in contrast to what we truly need. They prefer us to be our *normal selves* and try to get us back to that point as quickly as possible. *Trust yourself.*

All emotions have a message and grief was speaking loud and clear. It reminded me pain is always part of healing and the throbbing was a sign of unfinished business—unaddressed grief that was still trying to heal. Throbbing is a sign of repair that occurs when increased blood flow is directed to an area that has been damaged. So, from an emotional standpoint, the felt sense of pain is an important part of the process and much more adaptive than feeling numb and disconnected.

It felt like the day would never end, but as I crawled into bed a few final tears slid down my face. I whispered up toward the sky, "Happy birthday Mom. I miss you." I looked forward to the joy that would come in the morning.

Without a doubt, this experience was compounded by all the other boulders on my chest. These boulders are an accumulation of what we carry. This can be anything from the demands of life and new endeavors to the pressures of the present and uncertainty of the future. Some of us also carry deep hurt and every bad thing that has happened in our lives. We all carry something, but when the load becomes too heavy it will make it extremely difficult to move. The weight of these boulders can create a level of exhaustion that will limit our vision, maintain our doubt, and make every decision a struggle.

The emotional pressure and weight we carry can burden our nervous system and keep survival mode on deck. This means we will do whatever it takes to make what pains us stop but give little thought to how our survival tactics impact our future. Operating out of this burdened mindset is like having our wind knocked out and expecting to stand back up and keep going. *This is not happening!*

Our breath is the life force that keeps our energy flowing, increasing our endurance to engage in patterns that align with our goals. How we manage our burdens and make shifts that will balance the load will directly influence how much energy we have left for ourselves. Let's look at three of the most common ways we manage our boulders of burden and the *eviction* practices than can help lighten our emotional load.

* * * *

THE "PERFECT" FIT

First, we attempt to hold on to every boulder, believing we have no other choice. We convince ourselves we can figure out a way to stack them, making the pain bearable. We believe we are the only ones who can carry this load, and if we aren't careful, we take pride in being a martyr. On the other hand, we live life walking on eggshells, afraid at any moment things will fall apart.

Jeremy was a client who struggled to believe he had any another option than managing his pain by letting it all build up. This was a habit of coping he adopted when his father left and he, at ten years old, decided to be the man of the house. As a child he became protective and well attuned to the emotional needs of his mother and siblings, doing all he could to help them remain hopeful and happy. Now in his early thirties, he was depressed, exhausted, and unhappy. Jeremy was convinced to be present for others meant he couldn't be there for himself.

Our work centered around Jeremy's identity and how his value was attached to caring for others at the expense of himself. He uncovered his iceberg, recognizing the strength and fortitude he would outwardly exude and how it masked the overwhelm and inner struggles he carried.

We set small action steps to help Jeremy challenge his beliefs in over productivity and discover what it meant to make himself a priority. Jeremy was able to experience the discomfort of vulnerability and even attract people in his life that cared for him, regardless of his ability to be useful to them. It was powerful to watch Jeremy's view of himself shift and translate in a sustainable sense of self-worth that was no longer centered on being everyone else's hero.

* * * *

YOU HAVE TO SEE IT TO BELIEVE IT

Another common pattern is to ignore the weight of our boulders, despite the clear signs of damage. We are the walking wounded and either expect others to clean our wounds or we hurt others along the way. When this is the mentality, we use our pain to get attention but push them away if they try and hold us accountable. There is no intention of doing things differently because that would require us to admit our wrong. Instead, we overcompensate and tell ourselves the pain we carry will eventually go away. At all costs, we stay in a place of denial, discredit our exhaustion, and place everyone around us at risk.

This reminds me of my work with Sarah, who could see the evidence of destructive damage in her life, but not through a clear lens. She struggled to ever feel settled or content, with a constant need to stay busy and on the go. This even impacted her sleep, which created challenges with her mood and memory, but resting made her feel guilty.

Sarah admittedly loved the idea of having a family, but not necessarily being with her family. She thought her children were fun and helped her create connections in the community, but she would find herself overwhelmed and annoyed if she was "stuck at home with them too long."

Her husband and children showed signs of frustration, but she felt only performative remorse. In other words, Sarah would only make small changes and just long enough to temporarily extinguish the fire her patterns created.

During the course of our time together, Sarah and I took time to trace and uncover the progression of her behaviors and what it was like to live in a place of constant discontent. Sarah came to realize her pace was her primary means of managing her anxiety of not being enough for her family. She connected this belief to the messages she witnessed between her parents, who eventually divorced. Staying busy and having something to look forward to was Sarah's way of limiting her connection to her family, believing it would make it easier if they ever decided to leave.

Once Sarah had the words to describe her internal experiences, she chose to share them with her husband, which helped him support her and no longer feel he was the source of her disappointment.

In sessions, we practiced grounding techniques to help Sarah tolerate the physical aspects of her anxiety and urges to flee situations that felt like a threat. Grounding techniques can be as simple as slowing down the pace of the breathing or looking around the room and audibly describing the colors and names of objects within the space. These activities help balance the intensity of what's being felt and help us recognize strong physical sensations, that when given time, will slowly decrease on their own.

Over time, Sarah learned how to be present and to trust that the people in her life were not giving indicators they would leave. Her anxiety subsided and her thoughts shifted into a more neutral outlook on her ability to be loved.

One of the most beautiful sentiments she expressed was, "I simply had no idea that the sense of peace and security I so desperately craved was surrounding me all along."

* * * *

CAVE DWELLER

Some of us take our boulders and create a cave to escape. We keep all our struggles close by and stack them up. When we operate out of this mindset, we give very little thought to our power of choice. Sadly, our difficulties hold a source of comfort we often deny. In our mind, we justify shutting down and believe we aren't strong enough to resist this response pattern. What makes this one of the most damaging patterns is that the more you retreat, the more you reinforce the habit and each time it becomes more difficult to find your way back to the light.

Lee was a junior in college and over the past three years he had consistently seen changes in his typical behavior. Although he enjoyed college, it created a constant source of pressure and the only way he felt it could be managed was to withdraw. During his sophomore year, he began taking long daily naps, but convinced himself it was typical college behavior. Social settings were now so uncomfortable, they impacted his ability to attend class and secure internships for the coming summer.

When Lee thought about graduating and having to be out and among people every day, he would become nauseous and at times physically ill. His habit of avoidance had become suffocating and now stood in the way of his future.

During our first session, Lee asked if better was possible because this wasn't how he wanted to live. He had some incredible aspirations and didn't want his fears to stand in the way of achieving his dreams and helping others. Lee said, "I know I can have a positive impact and it's that same knowledge that scares me, paralyzes me, and backs me into a corner."

Lee's mindset was stuck in *all or nothing thinking,* which would always lead him to the worst case scenario. When you engage in all or nothing thinking, you view life in extremes that are black and white. You're either a success or failure; life is either great or a disaster.

When this is the predominant mindset, retreating will often seem like the safest option. Lee's underlying belief was the demand for perfection, which often derailed his attempts to help himself. Rigidity and criticism were Lee's sources of motivation and had to be unlearned. He was attached to his failures and thought keeping them fresh in his mind would decrease the chances they would happen again.

One of our first steps was helping Lee learn to balance the amount of pressure he placed on himself. We identified what circumstances caused his internal pressure to intensify and what beliefs were attached to these feelings. Then, we identified how he could shift the language he used toward himself, creating some flexibility in his desire to be perfect. For example, he went from "if I am not the best at what I do, I've failed" to "proceeding with excellence means learning from my mistakes."

Lee also needed to learn and understand the value of self-compassion—how to move from harsh judgment to being kind to himself. Making this shift helped Lee challenge perfectionism and realize he could accomplish his goals without being tough on himself. He also noticed his anxiety decreased and he regained confidence in social situations.

I don't believe any of us intend to carry our failures from one season to the next, but once we begin, it can be difficult to stop. If you're like Lee, keeping a record of wrong has become a fortress, and you start to suffocate. Remaining close to your pain won't keep you from falling into the same traps because our struggles aren't a dependable shield. They weigh us down and make our lives more difficult than necessary. We must constantly *evict the remnants of our regrets, so we maintain an attitude of hope and optimism.*

Where are you holding on to too tight?

* * * *

Eviction practices are fueled by consistency and help you operate out of a higher place of potential and develop the habits to sustain your growth. Consider how these practices and principles can become an organic part of your daily life. If you modify your consistency, you modify your progress.

BE YOUR OWN ACTIVIST

Caring for ourselves is a form of activism and has yet to hold its rightful place of priority.

Somewhere along the way caring for ourselves has been misinterpreted as a luxury, as if it's a privilege to take care of the one body and one mind we are given. One of our primary problems is our narrow concept of care that has been reduced to spa days and buying ourselves gifts.

Don't get me wrong, I am all for team "treat yo'self," but I am speaking from a different place of reference. Without much opposition, we have allowed consumerism to develop wellness into a construct that centers around products and privileged access to wellness spaces. However, if you understood the historical evolution of wellness, you would likely reduce the value you place on the concept.

Activism, for our purposes, can be viewed as the use of direct and noticeable action to achieve a result. Being your own activist means leaning into self-discovery and intentionally supporting your intended trajectory. By nature, activists also concern themselves with the social, economic, and environmental changes necessary for reform (Treleaven, 2018).

People often struggle to apply the concept of personal activism. It is not a visualization exercise where you imagine your best self and walk around wondering if this dream will come true. Personal activism is a direct, bold, and tangible effort that is founded in balance. You focus directly on your goals and give equal value to the ways you develop and engage in the process of change.

Self-activism allows us to engage in our lives without sacrificing what's most important. It means we give ourselves permission to develop our own personal definition of well-being, while acknowledging our needs will evolve.

Operating from this mindset encourages us to maintain a high sense of self-awareness and to abandon the process of ignoring our personal needs. It means every single day we engage in the vital habits and pursue the relationships that not only support who we are, but who we are becoming. Imagine unapologetically pouring this level of effort into your growth.

What if we became mental activists tapping into the care of our mindset and determined to stop resisting our needs?

PRACTICE STILLNESS

Stillness gives us the space to make choices. It allows us to pause and decide how we want to respond. This reminds me of my first yoga class, which I admit was a struggle. It was so slow, and I wanted to move faster. In my head I questioned the value of flowing through the poses and planned what I would do after the class to satisfy the hard effort I craved. Then during the last five minutes of class the instructor led us into the final resting pose, known as Savasana. He asked a simple question that left a profound impact…

Can you allow yourself permission to be still?

Up until doing yoga, the only time I gave myself permission to practice stillness was when I was too sick to move or at night when I slept. In those few minutes I did give myself permission to be still, and I was amazed at what I was given back through my willingness to yield.

When I left the class my feelings about yoga had not immediately changed, but I told myself if I was that resistant to slowing my pace, then it was exactly what I needed. Even when we begin to see and experience possibility and potential, there will still be resistance to change. Surrendering to the wisdom of my Savasana experience became the catalyst for my personal meditation and yoga practice. I also went on to earn my five-hundred-hour yoga certification and have spent the last five years researching and studying how our body responds to both movement and stillness.

I've also adapted these principles into my work with clients who feel they align with their beliefs. Many have found it to be useful in expanding their ability to make choices. By incorporating small moments of stillness, guided meditation, and other mindfulness practices, my clients learn to recognize their ability to access a sense of calm and stillness at any moment. For those who ascribe to the Christian faith, they use these practices as a reminder to slow down and connect with God.

Mindfulness is also an evidence-based practice, backed by research, and culturally relevant to diverse populations. A 2016 Oxford University meta-analysis found mindfulness-based therapy was more effective at reducing depression relapses than antidepressant medication. There is power in stillness, but it requires us to lean into the initial discomfort and relinquish fears toward sitting with our truth.

In his book *The Miracle of Mindfulness,* Thich Nhat Hanh (1996) reminds us...

"Breath is the bridge which connects life to consciousness, which unites your body to your thoughts. Whenever your mind

becomes scattered, use your breath as the means to take hold of your mind again."

Practicing meditation helps us focus on the present moment and provides the nervous system a rest five times deeper than sleep (Treleaven 2018). Current clinical research also demonstrates meditation helps to enhance sleep, increase focus, and reduce emotional reactivity (Goleman and Davidson 2017). This can be achieved in as little as five to seven minutes a few times a week and the impact can be immediately experienced.

PROTECT YOUR ENERGY.

Protecting our energy requires us to take crown and cape in hand, throw it in the fire, and walk away from overload. We must know where to extend our efforts and where our efforts are being manipulated, abused, or taken for granted. Although we are relational beings designed for connection, not everyone should be given full access to our lives. This may even include family.

In order to open the mental space we need to establish new mindsets, a shift of perspective and habits is always required. We must choose to release what's no longer in our best interest and make room for more of what we want to invite. This also makes it important to protect ourselves during the transition and to create the conditions we need to solidify our growth.

Plants are often kept in a green house, protected from the elements until they are strong enough to withstand the unpredictable elements outside. In parallel, we want to be more selective of our environment and relationships. This does not mean hiding or avoidance but being more responsible for the way our connections can choke out our growth. It also means understanding the kind of relationship dynamics we attract and how they keep us caught in a cycle of disappointment.

When I approach this topic with clients, they often assume I am referring to boundaries. Protecting your energy often includes boundary setting, but that is a very small part of the process. Even brief interactions with the wrong people can have lasting consequences. It is much like the belief that ships don't sink because of the water around them; ships sink because of the water that gets in them.

Pay close attention to your interactions and how they create any level of disruption in your life. Sometimes people may pull from you in direct ways, but also in subtle and unanticipated ways such as preying on your vulnerabilities and needs.

If you are a person who finds great value in being there for others, people can manipulate your kindness. They slowly and deliberately drain your energy, but quickly show their unwillingness to support your needs. There's a time to be a nice person and a time to say enough is enough. Sometimes we need to announce this to others, and sometimes we need to say this to ourselves.

Our greatest battles are often self-imposed. We battle impulsivity, poor work ethic, inconsistency, or even being passive. Don't accept this display of mediocrity or sitting on the sidelines because you can't keep pace with your purpose. The demands of discipline will match the magnitude of your purpose, so if you feel you're trailing behind, make adjustments.

Steve Maraboli, a decorated military veteran and author of *Unapologetically You*, makes a powerful statement: *"Sometimes it's the same moments that take your breath away that breathe purpose and love back into your life."*

RESTORE:

<u>Reclining Bound Angle Pose</u> *Positioning and finding surrender in a restorative pose allows your connective tissues, nervous system, and muscles to release tension and helps to calm and reset both the body and mind. This is an invitation to practice stillness. Feel free to substitute this posture for any other restorative pose that better suits your body's needs.*

Remember, this is optional and here to enhance your experience. If this mindfulness practice becomes uncomfortable at any time, honor your need to stop.

Start by lying down on your back. (Mat, floor, or bed)

Bend the knees and begin with your heels flat, then pull your feet as close as possible to your pelvis.

Slowly open your knees and allow them to fall to the sides, making the soles of the feet touch. (If you can.)

Put bolsters, blocks, or pillows under both knees so the stretch in your inner thighs doesn't feel too intense. (Honor your body's flexibility without judgment)

You can open your arms out to the sides or rest the hands on your belly.

Relax and let go of every part of your body, connecting with the surfaces supporting your frame and drawing your attention to the rise and fall of your breathing.

Stay here for at least five minutes with steady, slow breathing. (Eyes open or closed)

Optional: If silence is challenging, choose binaural or ambient music to play softly in the background.

REFLECT:

Describe the different ways you manage your past regrets and present pressures.

What needs to end or be silenced to better protect your mind?

What relationships need to be reframed or severed to support your growth? How do you honestly feel about the changes that need to be made?

If you stop and take inventory of your current season of life, what does it reveal about how you actively care for yourself?

RECALIBRATE:

The Mindset: No matter what I do, people constantly let me down.

*Use the space below to develop a **mental shift** to help recalibrate your perspective on the mindset above:*

Strengthen Your Frame

---

*The Mindset: I don't have the
energy to invest in myself.*

I've recently become a faithful Peloton rider. It has not only been a great way to manage my stress, but also an unexpected source of inspiration and knowledge. While taking a themed ride called "Speak Up" with the instructor, Tunde Oyeneyin, she made a powerful statement...

"Movements are the story of how we come together when we've come apart."

There can be a beautiful chaos in the contradiction between coming together while coming apart. Effectively navigating chaos requires the joint participation of both our mind and body. This isn't always as easy as it sounds. There are days when the thought of doing more than getting up and making it to the couch can be in direct opposition with what we consider valuable.

I can vividly remember days where my "best" meant putting on matching clothes and anything beyond that was a miracle. When we feel like we are coming apart, the absolute last thing we may want to do is *move*. Nevertheless, inner work and outer shifts, or new patterns of action, can be valuable allies that prevent our shadow's attempt at overpowering our light.

Over the past decade there has been growing research emphasizing the importance of the body in restoring the impaired connection between our mind and body (Menakem 2017). The science is finally catching up to what life has shown us all along. If we stop and pay attention, our connections to ourselves and others have a long and rich history of trying to get our attention.

A well-functioning mind to body connection is like the groove of the harmonies in your favorite song. It keeps us in tune with ourselves and with those we love. This is why grief and loss of our attachments can so easily stop us in our tracks.

＊ ＊ ＊ ＊

After the death of my mother, caring for my children literally kept my body moving. It set the pace and direction for my day, giving certainty to what was next. On the days that moving felt impossible, the needs of my children helped give me the motivation to come together when my heart was coming apart. This is only one small example of the strength they unknowingly poured into my frame. I can no longer keep count of the number of times they were the catalyst that willed me to fight and the calm that kept me from being consumed. My heart warms and my eyes become soft each time they come to mind.

Due to various medical complications, I was told conceiving a child would be extremely difficult and may not happen. I was blessed with the gift of carrying life, unaware of how these same lives would carry me in their hearts and smiles along the way. My children were my guiding light and gave way to purpose when life felt dark.

When *my mind and body felt at odds*, they were the bridge. They are now and will forever be the most dynamic movements in my story.

Life will crash in and repeatedly threaten to challenge the strength of our frame. It will tempt us to either abandon connection with our physical body or become punitive and rigid as an attempt to regain control. Yet, our body wants nothing more than to stay in balance. It is not your opponent and takes no pride in your frustrations. It does not love you more on some days and less on others.

Our bodies try to manage the experiences that incite and attack our stability, create threats, and activate duress. We can engage our body through avenues that teach it to release and allow this activation to move through, returning the body to a deep place of rest and support (Parker 2020). This state of rest increases our ability to be present and helps reduce our need to detach from the physical symptoms of suffering.

Contrary to what many people recognize, trauma is not solely an emotional response; it always happens in the body (Menakem 2017). Physical movement helps the nervous system develop a buffer, which enhances our ability to strengthen our psychological immune system (Parker 2020). This further supports the benefit of a multidimensional approach to piercing through our shadow and stepping into a higher place of potential.

There is expressed value in body-based compassion and engaging in approaches that support healing in the mind through healing in the body. Addressing the role of the body and engaging through movement is an often overlooked and underutilized approach to our well-being (NurrieStearns 2013).

While not specifically the focus of this moment, I do want to mention the value of body-based therapies that focus on the way emotions are stored within the body. These approaches are effective supports for addressing concerns such as stress, addiction, athletic performance, body image, anxiety, depression, trauma, and so much more.

Here are some body-based therapies I highly recommend:

- Brainspotting
- EMDR
- Embodied Recovery (specifically for eating disorders)
- Sensorimotor Therapy
- Somatic Experiencing
- Yoga

* * * *

Nikki Myers is a yoga therapist and teacher, somatic experiencing practitioner, and founder of Yoga of 12 Step Recovery

(Y12SR). Her teaching emphasizes, "Anything that lies in the body unresolved, unprocessed, unfinished, incomplete can cause difficulties and toxins later." After battling addiction, years of recovery, and then two relapses, Nikki realized that movement was an essential aspect of sustaining recovery and the missing component to her cognitive work.

Through the work of Y12SR, Nikki speaks of the ways in which yoga has helped improve her relationship with trauma and embrace acceptance instead of shame. Our relationship with trauma is like a game of hide and seek, where we repeatedly experience anything hidden until it is brought into awareness.

Her work offers a tangible and practical perspective toward overcoming substance and behavioral-based addictions.

Y12SR is a holistic model that addresses the physical, mental, and spiritual dis-ease of addiction. Informed by the latest research in neuroscience and trauma healing, Y12SR "connects the dots" by combining the somatic approach of yoga with the cognitive approach of the 12-step recovery model— the most well-known addiction recovery program in the world, with millions of active practitioners (Myers 2012).

While attending one of her trainings on breaking the barriers of codependency, I had a personal experience that further developed my thoughts toward the role of movement and its ability to transform both our mind and body.

The room was warm and colorful, filled with a sea of diverse bodies. An aroma of acceptance and gratitude seemed to fill the air, allowing each of us to honor our body without comparison. Lying on my back with my eyes gazing toward the window, I positioned my hands where my palms faced up. We entered a time of stillness, and I could feel each vertebra of my body begin to yield.

Nikki took us through a yoga practice that was a series of very simple and intricate movements completed in sequence and paced with our breath. I allowed myself to relinquish any judgment around my own body's capabilities. What amazed me was the sense of freedom and relief in my body and how it was enhanced through each posture.

In meeting my body at its place of need, I was nourished and rejuvenated. As we moved into a time of conscious conversation, my mind felt open and clear. The internal mental chatter I initially carried into the room was now replaced with a sense of clarity and peace. Mindful movement helps create a resilient nervous system, allowing us to engage through calm when navigating distress.

The ability to move our bodies is both a privilege and necessary aspect of sustaining well-being. If we abuse this privilege through overuse, we can incur injuries that result in pain and loss of use. If we underutilize the privilege of moving our body, stiffness and immobility can develop. It can also increase our risk for developing concerns such as high cholesterol, heart disease, and diabetes (Parker 2020).

Appropriately incorporating movement creates a powerful balance between activity, rest, and recovery, but some people view it as a villain or source of personal punishment. This view is founded in a competitive nature of body comparison and reducing exercise to a means of controlling body shape and size.

What do you notice about your internal response when you think about exercise?

* * * *

If your immediate response to exercise is filled with feelings such as disgust, avoidance, fear, or failure, this part of your being is in need of repair. When we find the balance of physical activity that works for our individual body, it can support our mental health in several ways. Exercise performed at moderate intensity releases neurotransmitters that increase blood flow, improve brain functioning, and improve mood (Deslandes et al. 2009).

A narrow mindset toward movement can keep us fighting against our potential, staying in a place of resistance to the key practices we may need. Exercise, when used appropriately, is a vital and complementary support to improving our mental health and mindset. It is also one of the core values I explore with clients presenting with depression.

Depression is one of the most commonly diagnosed mental health disorders, and according to the most recent research by the National Alliance on Mental Illness (NAMI), nineteen million four hundred thousand adults are diagnosed with major depression and forty-eight million adults battle anxiety. True to many mental health conditions, the impact of depression is far reaching and not confined to our mental functioning. Depression contributes to our physical distress and overall health, impairing our quality of life and general functioning (Elbe et al. 2019).

When depressed, most people believe sleep is one of the primary ways to find relief. While rest is extremely valuable to our bodies, too much time in a dormant state can increase our feelings of depression. Moreover, we typically use sleep to avoid our problems, ignoring the fact that our problems and challenges will still be there when we wake up.

* * * *

When Jade, a twenty-year-old college student, battled depression, I did not tell her to go become a runner to heal. We discussed her emotions and how they influence changes in her activity level.

On average, Jade spent about twelve to fourteen hours a day sleeping, which made her more tired and increased her anxiety around having less time to complete her work. The next step for each client depends on several factors. I evaluate areas such as the client's relationship with food, body image, comorbid medical conditions, and even past injuries or negative experiences.

We also explored family or origin messages that impact these areas as well as any current dynamics that directly influence their overall mind-body experience. One of my primary goals is to educate clients on how movement supports the nervous system, which supports our emotions and cognitive efforts.

Exercise increases several neurotransmitters, such as serotonin (5-HT) which stabilizes our mood, dopamine (D) which allows us to feel pleasure, acetylcholine (ACh) a key component of our nervous system, and norepinephrine (NE) which plays a significant role in our ability to focus (Schultz 2013). Together, we are then able to begin a road map that will set up the conditions needed for mind – body balance. When our bodies are in a state of arousal that is too high or low, it can block our ability to access and adjust our mindsets (Van Der Kolk 2014).

* * * *

Jeffrey Witherspoon is a US Army Battalion Commander (Airborne) at the 5th Special Forces Group and has dedicated his life to both serving our country and his local community. He is a certified hand-to-hand combat instructor and has served multiple tours in Iraq. Commander Witherspoon is not one of my clients, but has a powerful story that demonstrates his resilience, humility, and heart for helping others.

He also has a natural hunger for learning, which was further enhanced during his time at The Citadel and later at the College of William and Mary where he received his MBA while still on active duty. When you meet and interact with the commander, it's evident his traumas are not at the forefront of his mindset, leading from a place of pain. He comes across with an authentic balance of strength and energy that gently invites respect.

The commander and I initially met online through a mutual acquaintance. He was the founder of an online fitness group committed to improving mind-body health. Every evening he would log on and offer education and motivation for thousands of individuals working to improve their health. This was more than a business; it was a movement. Diverse individuals from across the world were positively engaged in and supportive of each other's collective goals.

While I have come across dozens of individuals who focus on well-being, there was something special about his level of passion and conviction. His mental mindset was an intricate part of his belief system, and it became evident this was an extension of his personal life. My in-person interactions with the commander and his wife Danielle further solidified my thoughts.

During our interview, Commander Witherspoon shared that as a young man he was determined to use his challenges to fuel his sense of purpose, instead of allowing them to create doubt. There was a clear and present conviction in his words and a look of excitement in his eyes.

He shared, "Life did not afford me the privilege of having a lot of safety nets, so it wasn't easy for me to give up or to quit. I had to learn to push through when times were tough. Failure was not an option."

My intent was to protect the commander's privacy, so I didn't probe further, but imagined the overwhelm of making such a strong determination as a young man working to defy the odds. As he continued to share, I inwardly smiled and thought, even before he was a soldier he was learning how to fight.

His story reminded me life will bring challenges and there will be times when giving up seems easier than pushing forward. Each of these moments is also an avenue for growth, but the outcome will largely depend on the strength of our frame and the power of our mindset.

* * * *

The "strength of our frame" is both tangible and metaphorical. Our body is the only vehicle we have to engage in life. It is directly involved in every aspect of our existence, allowing us to move throughout our day, experience intimacy and connection, and it guards and protects our vital life systems.

Strengthening our frame not only provides an adaptive way to develop whole body health and manage stressors, but also creates a level of fortitude necessary for survival. It tolerates our inconsistencies and forces us to take the rest we would otherwise sacrifice.

Metaphorically, the strength of our frame helps override our impulses and extends support during our challenges. It preserves our power and can turn the tide of our will when we least expect it. A body in a depressed state can, on in its own, come back into balance, slowly reopening the pathway for us to once again experience joy. Our bodies are an intricate framework, acting as a conduit with expansive range and attuning to our ever-changing needs. *Even when we war against our bodies and treat them with neglect, they will do all they can to save our lives.*

In his own life, Commander Witherspoon learned to harness the power between mind and body. One of the toughest aspects of his life came through active combat. These experiences required a strong reliance on his instinct and an even stronger commitment to not losing himself in the process.

"You have to have a certain mindset and mentality to be brave enough to go into that situation and not second guess or get afraid. If you are afraid and question your judgment, that could be someone's life." He went on to explain, "The casualties of combat don't end when the battle stops, leaving many combat veterans working to turn off the aggressive mentality you need in combat and become the gentle and loving person your family needs."

After seeing so many soldiers struggle to manage their stress and the demands of combat, the commander became determined to find a healthy way to cope. "I had to find a way to positively control my thoughts, feelings, and my emotions." This led him to the gym and exercise became his "release valve." Jeff quickly noticed, "Being alone in the gym was my time of solitude, to brain dump and to lift the troubles of the day off my shoulders. It's almost like lifting the weights was physically removing stressors off my back. When I feel strong and disciplined in my body, I feel this same degree of strength in my mind."

The strength we feel in our body can absolutely influence our mind in a positive manner. Exercise is a proven non-pharmacological approach to enhancing the subcortical areas of the brain where traumatic memories are stored and rational processing takes place (Deslandes et al. 2009). When our quality of life is highly efficient, we are more likely to make better decisions. However, this is not mutually exclusive.

We can abuse exercise and while presenting with a high level of external discipline, our internal world may be crumbling. *Balance is essential and cultivating this equilibrium* requires us to take consistent inventory of what we need and what is no longer in our best interest. When we commit to the *joint process of addressing both our physical frame and mental framework, it increases our felt sense of power.*

You move differently when you understand your power.

* * * *

The commander's combat experiences undeniably place him at high risk for post-traumatic stress disorder (PTSD). PTSD can develop when we experience or witness life-threatening and highly distressing incidents such as military combat, accidents, assault, or even when living through crisis or natural disasters (Hegberg, Hayes, & Hayes 2019).

PTSD is a prominent mental health problem, especially in veterans and community populations that are the victims of repeated acts of violence and trauma (NAMI, 2021). While these are the most common dynamics, anyone can experience PTSD, including children. It can also occur after serious accidents, after experiences of physical and sexual assault, and even through vicarious exposure situations where we remotely see a triggering event.

Throughout his military tenure, the commander experienced and witnessed the impact of unresolved and suppressed combat stress. It opened his eyes to the reality of psychological stress faced on and off the battlefield. As a result, the commander continues to support and encourage those battling PTSD and looking for guidance on how to shift their connection toward mind-body health. Living in a constant state of survivor mode is not as empowering as it has been made to sound.

Survivor mode can be analogous to operating from a place of dysfunctional connection. In this state we often engage in habits and thought patterns that work against our long-term health and prevent our mind and body from operating in balance. Everything becomes a reaction and a plot to avoid our perceived threats, which can feel like everything when we are overwhelmed.

This mindset can be steeped in deception, and we often minimize personal care or justify the potential for harm by avoiding the reality of our physical state. Operating from this mindset may involve practices such as inconsistently meeting our nutritional needs, not getting enough sleep, and avoiding signs of physical or emotional distress.

We are designed to work in harmony and our emotional and physical health collectively influence our sense of well-being. Our neuromuscular system is the integrated exchange between our nervous system and muscle control. This means our emotions will impact our physical state, regardless of our body size. Spending time building our emotional and physical well-being must never be optional.

It is one thing to be aware of our vulnerabilities, but another thing to both identify and put in place the practices that will reduce the degree of potential harm. As expert researcher and addictions specialist Dr. Gabor Mate affirms, "When you shut down emotions, you're also affecting your immune system and your nervous system. So, the repression of emotion, which is a survival strategy then becomes a source of physiological illness later on." Look at where you are and envision what it means to take the next step forward.

You are your greatest investment.

RESTORE:

LEGS UP A WALL
This restorative pose is an inversion that is a powerful reminder that less is more. It helps restore blood flow into areas of your body that don't typically get attention. This is an invitation to practice stillness. Feel free to substitute this posture for any other restorative pose that better suits your body's needs. Remember, this is optional and here to enhance your experience. If this mindfulness practice becomes uncomfortable at any time, honor your need to stop.

Precautions

(If you have any discomfort in your lower back, move your body slightly back from the wall. Or if you have any neck strain, you can place a small rolled-up blanket, towel, or flat pillow underneath.)

- Place a folded blanket a few inches from the wall. The distance of your placement from the wall will depend on your tightness and height.
- Lie down on the floor by rolling your hips onto the blanket.
- Now adjust your body against the wall by raising your legs.
- Arms can be gently placed on your belly, by your side with palms facing up or down, or for a chest opener, out to the side like goal posts. Do whatever feels good for you.
- Allow yourself to get comfortable and then choose a soft gaze or close your eyes while you release and let go.

REFLECT:

How is your current relationship with your body? Think in terms of both your strengths and areas of need.

Describe the different ways your body responds when you're in a place of high distress?

Investing in yourself means you're worth the time and effort. What's the difference between the investment you make in others versus the ways you invest in yourself?

RECALIBRATE:

The Mindset: I don't have the energy to invest in myself.

*Use the space below to develop a **mental shift** statement that will help recalibrate your perspective:*

You Are Still There

Sitting with my clients is an experience I don't take for granted. While we all have the opportunity for growth, our access to tangible support is not equal.

One morning in my office, I had a moment I fully believe was inspired by God.

There, in the stillness, an undercurrent of emotion filled the room, and I wrote these words below. These words echo a message I want to extend to you.

"You Are Still There"

My heart beats deeply for your pain.
As I sit and feel your energy and your words fill the space.
I see you and I am not afraid.
You can bring all of who you are and in that
moment I will hold it, protect it, respect it.
So, speak.
Speak freely and without fear, allowing
all that you've held inside to rise.

Speak. Break free from the pain of your past.
I see HOPE.
I see PROMISE.
I see HEALING.
And in the midst of the desperation, I
feel what is buried deep within.
You are still there, hiding inside.
The path may be filled with twists, and
turns, and disappointment.
But I implore you not to give up. There is hope.
It takes courage to rise and face the day.
I honor your fight, even when those closest cannot see it.
YOU. ARE. ENOUGH.
You have always been enough.
But this can never be fully recognized without
understanding and allowing yourself to
grasp the love from your Creator.
So speak.
Speak freely and without fear, allowing
all that you've held inside to rise.
Speak. Break free from the pain of your past.
I see you.
I am listening.
Yes, I am here.
Sitting quietly
Matching your breath and
Honoring your pace.
I am not afraid of your pain.
And nothing is too great for our God.

~ Charryse Johnson

CH.14

Rise from the Ashes

———

You may think I wrote this book for everyone, but it was written just for **you.**

I was intentional in my efforts to create clarity, yet leave space, and before asking to see your story, I was deliberate in sharing some of mine. Even more than I trust in the benefit of knowledge, I trust in the power of honoring our imperfections. There were no steps or formulas because you, my friend, cannot be reduced to an equation.

My hope is that some part of you felt seen—perhaps even a little understood. While there is nothing new under the sun, sometimes we can hear what we've always known in a way that finally makes it click. Keep reading, learning, and listening until you not only find what you need but also can allow it to land.

"We read to know we are not alone" is a quote from *Shadowlands,* a powerful film on humanity, love, and suffering. If I have done my job, you will leave these pages knowing you are not alone. There are hundreds, maybe thousands of other souls reading these pages. We may look different, live different, and have different beliefs, but there is one universal truth: All of us experience pain and have the same shade of red running through our veins. Our struggles remind us we are more alike than different.

When we are young, we choose safety as a natural mechanism to protect our spirit. However, as we mature, we must choose suffering, or the lessons that can only be learned as we walk through the fire. *So, if you continue the work beyond these pages, you will have moments that ache. You will grieve the loss of your habits and the self-defeating thoughts that have been painful, but also provided comfort.*

Much like the process of building new muscle, you will feel soreness in the fibers of your being, as they are torn down and rebuilt. But the new muscle will be better—stronger. The pain we experience now is a part of the power and potential we will feel later.

That's the deal. Our sadness helps us to appreciate joy and our low moments force us to stop, look up, and climb toward higher ground.

On my left arm I have a tattoo of a phoenix, a mythical bird known for rising from the ashes. According to legend, the phoenix goes through a cycle where it burns to death and is reborn from its own ashes. Confident it will rise, the phoenix does not fear the fire, but coasts boldly into the hottest part of the flames. Each time a phoenix emerges from the fire it is smarter, stronger, and more powerful than before. It represents our ability to rise to the challenge, determined to succeed.

Whatever challenges are behind you, around you, or those that are ahead, don't be afraid. Remember who you are. Remember when you considered giving up and decided to try one more time. Or when you found the courage to walk away, believing better was ahead than what you left behind. Remember that your tears are a sign of healing, not a sign of weakness. Remember that everyone's body needs deep rest, even yours.

You have made it through every fire that has come your way and the future will not be different. Like the phoenix, coast boldly into each day. I'm completely confident that you will.

RISE FROM THE ASHES!

Love,

Charryse

Acknowledgments

——

First and foremost, I want to thank God who has always been my ultimate source of strength and support. He is the source of the love I have for others and has blessed me in ways I don't deserve.

Thank you to all my interviewees and clients who gave up your time and shared your stories. To the beta readers who copiously read through my writing, your encouragement is an intricate part of this manuscript.

To my friends who held me up when I was tired and encouraged me along the way, thank you for staying connected and always checking in to make sure I was ok. Strong friends check on their strong friends, and for this I am eternally grateful.

A huge thank you to the team at New Degree Press, especially Benay Stein and Alayna Eberhart, who helped me find my voice as an author and cheered me on to the finish line. Eric Koester, your vision paved the way for my dream to become a reality. Thank you for laying the foundation and the passion you bring to the table.

Finally, to my husband Randy: You have been my lover, my soulmate, and my anchor for more than half my life. I am constantly amazed at the way you support my dreams and give me the space to develop my creative passions. Without your steadiness, I would not have started or finished this project. The cliché says behind every man is a good woman, but I believe *beside every great woman is a loving man.*

Special thanks to all the amazing individuals who supported this journey during the prelaunch campaign:

Aaron Pellot	Ashkea C Pee	Carrrie Ray
Abby Pepper	Ashlee Wright	Lisa Chambers
Amanda Lancaster	Ashley Cramer	Charlease Deathridge
Amy Marcum	Ashley Parker	
Amy Moore	Beth McLamb	Chelsea Ann Baron
Amy Obrien	Bobbie Evans	Cheryl Chastain
Amy Smith	Brandee Steward	Cheryl Pepper
Andrea Leverett	Cameron Toman	Cheryl Pepper
Angel Howell	Candice Coleman	Cheryl Singleton
Angela Bullock	Cantrell Murray Frayer	Christy Maloney
Ann-Marie Gariepy		Christy Sigmon
Anya Gromova	Carla Sadler	Constance D Lee
April Dennis-Mack	Carol Daley Cook	Courtney Bustle

Crissy Fishbane

Cynthia Carver-Futch

Dacquin Curry

Daniel and Katrina Heath

Danielle Wolfe

Davena Mgbeokwere

DaviAnn Fearon

Dawn Stanton

Debbie Leahy

Deetria Bridges

Diana Pike

Douglas Scherer

Ebony Baxter

Elizabeth Abowd

Elizabeth Hassell

Elizabeth Mooney

Ellen Patterson

Eric Koester

Eric Spohn

Erica Spratley

Eva Richardson

Grady Tallington Jr

Gwendolyn Jones

Hannah Blanton

Heather Bowman

Ivey Amburgey

Jaclyn Weber

Jacob Danzig

Jametha Washington-Bowman

Jamie B Touchberry

Jamillah D Bynum

Jane Tune

Jarel Nixon

Jeanette Hornsby

Jeneen Anderson

Jennifer Conquest

Jennifer Ellis

Jennifer Fadare

Jennifer Kolb

Jenny Willis

Jessecia Rawls

Jessica Cooper

Jill Burns

Jodell White

Joy Martinez

Juliet Kuehnle

Juliette Belliard

karen.lloyd

Kate Dyksterhouse

Katelyn Sauder

Kelly Alvarado-Young

Kelly Cap

Kelly White

Kenneth Samuelson

Kimberlee Mander

Kimberly Phelps

Kristen Cudney

Kristin Smith

L. Kay Barker

Lamecia Eaddy

Latoya Pousa

Lattisha Jackson

Laura Ahl

Lauren Manderson

Lavinia Marshall

Linda Glusenkamp

Lindsey McIntyre

Lisa Gerard

Lisa Reinhardt

Lori Hurndon

Lori Moore

Lorraine Tavarez Lopez

Lucy Schultz

Luther R. Fisher

Maggie Klonsky

Mark Scriven

Mary Martha Felkner

Meagan Lee

Megan Agee

Melissa Bugaj

Melissa Gill

Michaela Simmons

Michelle Cakleu

Molly Hunt

Mona Davis

Nanine
Hartzenbusch
Fox

Natasha
Hemmingway

Nathalie Santa
Maria

Nicole Mastrando

Nicole Webb

Octavia N Scott

Opia Espinosa

Page Hull

Pamela Brewer

Pashaun Chisholm

Patrice Witcher

Patricia Cotham

Patricia Johnson

Penelope Pauley

Rachel Holzhauer

Rebecca Epp

Rebekah Talley

Rueben Johnson

Sandra J Hodges

Shannon Wilder

Shawn Futch

Sherry Evans

Shlesta Thomas

Sorina Ilioi

Stephanie O'Mara

Stephenie Frasher

Sudie Johnson

Suzan Thompson

Suzette Hickman

Tamla Oates-Forney

Tanecia Lee-Bailey

Tawana Turner

Tesa Conerly

Vanecia Carr

Veronica Cashwell

Vickie Smith

Vivian Grafton

Wanda J Baird

Wendy Speckman

Yesenia Mueller

Zebrena Glover

Appendix A

CHAPTER 1

Brown, Brené. *Rising Strong*. Manhattan: Penguin Random House, 2015.

CHAPTER 2

Barlow, David, Vincent Durand, and Stefan Hofmann. *Abnormal Psychology: An Integrative Approach*. Boston: Cengage Learning, 2018.

Michl, Petra, Thomas Meindl, Franziska Meister, Christine Born, Rolf Engel, Maximillian Reiser, and Kristina Henning-Fast. "Neurobiological Underpinnings of Shame and Guilt: A pilot fMRI Study." *Social Cognitive and Affective Neuroscience* 2, no. 9 (2014): 150-7. doi:10.1093/scan/nss114.

Otegar, Henry, Mark Howe, Lawrence Patihis, Harald Merckelbach, Steven Lynn, Scott Lilienfeld, and Elizabeth Loftus. "The Return of the Repressed: The Persistent and Problematic Claims of Long-Forgotten Trauma." *Perspectives on Psycholog-*

ical Science 14, no. 6 (November 2019): 1072-1095. https://doi.
org/10.1177/1745691619862306.

CHAPTER 3

Asamen, Joy Keiko, Mesha L. Ellis, and Gordon L. Berry. *The SAGE
Handbook of Child Development, Multiculturalism, and Media.*
Thousand Oaks: Sage Publications, 2008.

Green, Christopher D. "Where Did Freud's Iceberg Metaphor of
Mind Come From?" *History of Psychology* 22, no. 4 (2019): 369-372.

Merriam-Webster.com Dictionary, s.v. "the tip of the iceberg,"
Accessed May 4, 202. https://www.merriam-webster.com/
dictionary/the%20tip%20of%20the%20iceberg.

Devine, Rory and Claire Hughes. "Relations Between False Belief
Understanding and Executive Function in Early Childhood:
A Meta-Analysis." *Child Development* 85, no. 5 (2014): 1777-794.
Accessed May 5, 2021. http://www.jstor.org/stable/24033017.

Daoshan, Ma and Zhang Shuo. "A Discourse Study of the Iceberg Principle in *A Farewell to Arms.*" *Studies in Literature
and Language* 8, no.1 (2014):80-84. https://doi.org/10.3968/j.
sll.1923156320140801.3918.

Moreland, Kim. "Just the Tip of the Iceberg Theory: Hemingway and Sherwood Anderson's "Loneliness"." *The Hemingway* Review 19, no. 2 (Spring, 2000): 47-56. http://eres.regent.
edu/login?url=https://www-proquest-com.ezproxy.regent.edu/
scholarly-journals/just-tip-iceberg-theory-hemingway-sher-
wood/docview/218949220/se-2?accountid=13479.

James, Richard and Burl Gilliland. *Crisis Intervention Strategies*. Boston: Cengage Learning, 2017.

Tossani, Eliana. "The Concept of Mental Pain." *Psychotherapy and Psychosomatics,* 83 (2013):67-73. https://doi.org/10.1159/000343003.

CHAPTER 6

Anderson, Eric, RN Carleton, M Diefenbach, and PKJ Han. "The Relationship Between Uncertainty and Affect." *Frontiers in Psychology* 12, no. 10 (November 2019) doi:10.3389/fpsyg.2019.02504.

Barlow, David, Vincent Durand, and Stefan Hofmann. *Abnormal Psychology: An Integrative Approach*. Boston: Cengage Learning, 2018.

Campbell, Celeste. "What Is Neuroplasticity." Accessed June 2, 2021. https://www.brainline.org/author/celeste-campbell/qa/what-neuroplasticity.

Fuchs, E., & Flügge, G. (2014). "Adult Neuroplasticity: More Than 40 Years of Research." *Neural Plasticity, 2014,* Article 541870. https://doi.org/10.1155/2014/541870.

Leaf, Caroline. *Switch on Your Brain: The Key to Peak Happiness, Thinking, and Health*. Grand Rapids: Baker Books, 2013.

Pedrelli, Paola et al. "College Students: Mental Health Problems and Treatment Considerations." *Academic Psychiatry: The Journal of the American Association of Directors of Psychiatric Residency Training and the Association for Academic Psychiatry.* vol. 39, no. 5 (2015): 503-11. doi:10.1007/s40596-014-0205-9.

Sapolsky, Robert. *Behave: The Biology of Humans at Our Best and Worst*. Manhattan: Penguin Books, 2017.

Stiles, Joan, and Terry L Jernigan. "The basics of brain development." *Neuropsychology Review* vol. 20, no. 4 (2010): 327-48. https://doi:10.1007/s11065-010-9148-4.

Taylor, Jill. *My Stroke of Insight: A Brain Scientist's Personal Journey*. New York: Viking Press, 2008.

Van Der Kolk, Bessel. *The Body Keeps the Score*. New York: Penguin Books, 2014.

CHAPTER 7

Grilo, Carlos and James Mitchell. *The Treatment of Eating Disorders: A Clinical Handbook*. New York: Guilford Press, 2010.

Mehler, Philip and Arnold Anderson. *Eating Disorders: A Guide to Medical Care and Complications 3rd edition*. Baltimore: John Hopkins University Press, 2017.

National Alliance for The Mentally Ill, U.S. National Alliance on Mental Illness NAMI. United States, 2002. Web Archive. https://www.loc.gov/item/lcwaN0000280/.

Solodov, Denis and Ilia Solodov. "Data Recovery in a Case of Fire-Damaged Hard Disk Drives and Solid-State Drives." *Forensic Science International: Reports* 3, (2021): 100199. https://doi.org/10.016/j.fsir.2021.100199.

CHAPTER 8

Barlow, David, Vincent Durand, and Stefan Hofmann. *Abnormal Psychology: An Integrative Approach.* Boston: Cengage Learning, 2018.

Tara Brach. "Real but Not True: Freeing Ourselves from Harmful Beliefs." November 6, 2016, 58:57. https://youtu.be/yn8c1ex_eWs

Cain, Ruby. "Courageous Learning about Race, Self, Community and Social Action." *Adult Learning* 23, no. 4 (2012): 201-205.

Patil, Indrajeet, Marta Calo, Federico Fornasier, Fiery Cushman, and Giorgia Silani. "The Behavioral and Neural Basis of Empathetic Blame." *Scientific Reports* 7, no. 5200 (2017): 1-14.

CHAPTER 9

Masters, Robert. *Bringing Your Shadow Out of the Dark: Breaking Free from the Hidden Forces That Drive You.* Boulder: Sounds True, 2018.

CHAPTER 10

Boyd, Ty. *The Million Dollar Toolbox: A Blueprint for Transforming Your Life & Your Career with Powerful Communication Skills.* Charlotte: Alexa Press, 2002.

Thurman, Chris. *Your Attitude: Out with the Bad, In with the Good.* Eugen: Wipf and Stock Publishers, 2021.

Liberman, Nira, Michael Sagristano, and Yaacov Trope. "The Effect of Temporal Distance on Level of Mental Construal." *Journal of Experimental Social Psychology* 38, no. 6 (2002): 523-534.

Menakem, Resmaaa. *My Grandmother's Hands: Racialized Trauma and the Pathway to Mending Our Hearts and Bodies.* Las Vegas: Central Recovery Press, 2017.

Van Der Kolk, Bessel. *The Body Keeps the Score.* New York: Penguin Books, 2014.

CHAPTER 11

Hanh, Thicht Nhat. *The Mircale of Mindfulness: An Introduction to the Practice of Meditation.* New York: Beacon Press, 1996.

Goleman, Daniel and Richard Davidson. *Altered Traits: Science Reveals How Meditation Changes Your Mind, Brain, and Body.* New York: Avery Publishing, 2017.

Maraboli, Steve. *Unapologetically You: Reflections on Life and the Human Experience.* Port Washington: A Better Today Publishing, 2013.

Treleaven, David. *Trauma Sensitive Mindfulness: Practices for Safe & Transformative Healing.* New York: W. W. Norton & Company, 2018.

CHAPTER 12

Menakem, Resmaaa. *My Grandmother's Hands: Racialized Trauma and the Pathway to Mending Our Hearts and Bodies.* Las Vegas: Central Recovery Press, 2017.

NurrieStearns, Mary and Rick NurrieStearnes. *Yoga for Emotional Trauma: Meditations and Practices for Pain and Suffering.* Oakland: New Harbinger Publications, 2013.

Parker, Gail. *Restorative Yoga for Ethnic and Race-Based Stress and Trauma*. Philadelphia: Singing Dragon, 2020.

Schultz, Wolftram. "Updating Dopamine Reward Signals." *Current Opinion in Neurobiology* 23, no. 2 (2013): 229-238.

Van Der Kolk, Bessel. *The Body Keeps the Score*. New York: Penguin Books, 2014.

Appendix B

RECOMMENDED BOOKS ON NEUROPLASTICITY

- *Breaking the Habit of Being Yourself: How to Lose Your Mind and Create a New One* by Dr. Joe Dispenza
- *My Stroke of Insight: A Brain Scientist's Personal Journey* by Jill Bolte Taylor
- *The Brain That Changes Itself: Stories of Personal Triumph from the Frontiers of Brain Science* by Norman Doidge
- *Anatomy of the Soul: Surprising Connections between Neuroscience and Spiritual Practices that Can Transform Your Life and Relationships* by Curt Thompson
- *The Brain That Changes Itself: Stories of Personal Triumph from the Frontiers of Brain Science* by Norman Doidge
- *The Power of Neuroplasticity* by Shad Helmstetter
- *The Stress-Proof Brain: Master Your Emotional Response to Stress Using Mindfulness & Neuroplasticity* by Melanie Greenberg
- *The Brain's Way of Healing: Remarkable Discoveries and Recoveries from the Frontiers of Neuroplasticity* by Norman Doidge

- *Neuroplasticity (MIT Press Essential Knowledge Series)* by Moheb Costandi
- *Switch on Your Brain: The Key to Peak Happiness, Thinking, and Health* by Dr. Caroline Leaf

Made in the USA
Columbia, SC
05 October 2023